"Run For Hope" is a truly captivating story of growing up in rural Afghanistan and Pakistan. Born in the city to an educated and progressive father, Atal began his education at a very young age. But the war with the Taliban interfered with his education and he was sent to live with relatives in the rural area. There, he experienced a culture that had not changed in a thousand years. As a young boy, he was deeply affected by the brutal and heartbreaking treatment of girls and women as household slaves and as property to be bartered away as payment for debt or protection from adversaries. He witnessed the rigid adherence to the culture's interpretation of Islam and the disdain for secular education, and he personally experienced the routine physical mistreatment of children. As a teenager, he experienced beatings and ostracism from the community because he dared to question the Islamic tenets and practices and to learn more about Christianity.

The author is a natural storyteller who will keep you engrossed from beginning to end. This book provides insight into an ancient tribal culture that still exists today in rural Afghanistan and Pakistan, and it should be required reading for those who would advocate foreign intervention in these countries, whether militarily or for altruistic purposes. The author endured violent assaults and rejection for his renunciation of the prevailing culture and his embracing of Christianity. His tenacity should be an inspiration, not only to Christians, but to all those who seek to change society for the improvement of the human condition."

—*Joanne M. Belovich, Ph.D. Professor and Chair of the Department of Chemical and Biomedical Engineering in Cleveland State University*

"Atal takes us directly into a culture that most Americans only hear about through the news media. The story is told from his voice as a young boy who is thrust into the reality of life in a war-torn country when his parents decide to move him to an uncle's house in a different village. His story exposes us to brutalities that he struggles to come to terms with. He is outcast by schoolmates for speaking a different dialect and accused of being an infidel because he came from an Afghanistan town with communist sympathizers. We are exposed to the treatment of women by fathers who view daughters as property. One of his cousins with whom he has formed a friendship is traded into an arranged marriage, and we are left appalled at how she is beaten and mistreated by her new family....and eventually found dead laying in a barn and covered with animal feces and urine.

Atal is subjected to extreme pressure to be molded into this culture with traditions that have existed for thousands of years. In school, he is taught the jihad view by his teachers, and the extremism that non-believers must die. Despite this, he is curious about other religions, exploring the forbidden world of Christianity resulting in repeated physical beatings and eventually driving him to become an outcast by his own family.

This story gives us a true understanding of how different our cultures are, but also give us a sliver of hope that if one boy has the courage to question these brutal traditions, perhaps there is a chance for change."

— *Vicki Nofziger, Civil Engineer in First Energy*

This is a non-fiction work. All of the characters, organizations, and events described in this book occurred in author's life and are not imaginary.

RUN FOR HOPE

Copyright © 2017 by Atal RM Aryan

Cover design by Go Media

Edited by Frank W. Lewis and Shirin Dixon

Published by Atal RM Aryan

For all the questions contact the author of the book by
atalrmaryan87@gmail.com

Library of Congress Cataloging –in– Publication Data has been applied

Printed and bound in United States of America

First printing June 2017

ISBN-10: 0-692-90383-6
ISBN-13: 978-0-692-90383-4

ABOUT THE AUTHOR

Atal RM Aryan, the author of "Run For Hope", is originally from Afghanistan. He came as a refugee to the United States of America, and he lives in the USA now.

RUN FOR

HOPE

Atal RM Aryan

Introduction

Afghanistan is a small country in the Middle East, surrounded by Tajikistan, Turkmenistan, China, Uzbekistan, Iran and Pakistan. The overwhelming majority of the thirty-five million citizens are Muslims, but after that, the country is astonishingly diverse for its size. Even the religious differences are significant.

There are two dominant ethnic groups, Pashtuns and Afghan-Persians, and they have very different cultures. Afghan-Persian communities, made up of Tajiks, Uzbeks, Hazaras and Iranians, follow mainstream Shia Islam. Afghan-Persians tend to live in cities, and are generally friendly with Iranian and European people. I am an Afghan-Pashtun, born in Kabul, and my story is set in the Pashtun villages where I spent most of my childhood.

Most Pashtuns are Sunnis and live in rural areas, making their living from animal husbandry and farming. They take great pride in their traditional way of life and their strict code, known as Pashtunwali. The strongest of its tenets include *melmastia* (hospitality), *badal* (vengeance), *zamaka*, (the right to protect one's property), *nanawatay* (mercy, if the wrong-doer humiliates himself) and *tang* (honor). There is a separate word, *tor*, for the honor of women. *Namus*, a woman's chastity, is extremely important.

Pashtunwali is the law among the Pashtun people who live along the twenty-five-hundred-kilometer border with Pakistan; the central government has little influence there. Some of the houses in the villages are quite large with high walls, but some Pashtuns live as nomads and sleep in tents. The men of both types of families carry guns all the time. Firearms are one of few exceptions to their general disdain for technology.

Few parents send their children to school other than a madrassa, or religious school. They believe that the world will end soon, and God will not care how educated a person is. There are madrassas in the cities too, but in the villages the lessons sometimes extend to jihad and the righteousness of fighting non-Muslim people. Children have no say in what they learn. In most families, Islam and village tradition is considered enough.

The laws can be harsh, especially for girls and women. If a man loses a tooth in a fight, for example, the law decrees that the culprit must offer a girl from his family that the victim, or a relative of his choosing, can marry. The girl cannot refuse. Once wed, she lives with her new family and is often treated badly as ongoing punishment for the lost tooth. In most such cases, she may see her own family only once a year, or perhaps not at all.

But if the girl's male blood relatives learn that she is being mistreated, they may seek revenge. Disputes like this can lead to many fights, and even deaths, and can span generations. This is another reason that boys are prized; a family's strength depends in large part on the number of men.

Village women usually fetch water at the natural springs called *gudar* and from the nearby rivers that flow from the mountaintops to carve out the valleys. This is a rare chance to leave the house and meet with other girls and women away from men, who are banned from these sites. At some villages, young men and women can meet each other during celebrations. Any other kind of meeting, however, can be dangerous. If a boy stops a girl to talk with her, it's considered shameful to her family. Her male relatives might kill her to prevent her from running away with the boy, which shames the whole village. Or they might kill the boy to avenge the family's loss of prestige.

If a boy and girl like each other and meet, without family approval, they can both be killed. All marriages are arranged.

My grandfathers and other relatives still live in the village called Mangal, which sits among hills, beautiful rivers and green fields. The people wear battered, loose-fitting traditional clothes. The old houses are surrounded by big walls

11

and have heavy, black, wooden doors. Some of the doors have slots, and if you walk through the village, you can see women's eyes looking at you. Villagers will ask you "Where did you come from" and "What is your grandfather's name?" If they recognize your grandfather's name, they might tell you that he was a great and brave person.

They will offer you food — bread, strong green tea and *gora,* an Afghani sweet — and invite you to eat with them in their fields. They will tear the bread with their calloused hands. For some special guests, they might cook some potatoes with rice. They will offer you milk, eggs and butter. If you are from the city, they will call you "city guy" and suggest that you grow a big mustache and beard, because men with little or no facial hair remind them of girls. They will advise you to wear a big hat, to show respect, and a long scarf to wear on your shoulder.

In 1963, when my father, Tarub Khan, was 14 years old, his father, Amer, sent him to live in the city of Kabul. This was for my father's protection; the family was involved in a dispute with another family in the village. My grandfather told my father to find his old friend, Mer Akbar, and stay with him. He also warned my father not to attend school in the city. He was concerned that too much education would turn his son against God and make him a "city guy." Carrying only a blanket and wearing wooden shoes, my father caught a ride on a truck that made the one-hundred-mile journey to Kabul every week.

He learned how hard this transition would be as soon as he arrived. Most residents of Kabul were Afghan-Persians, and they spoke Dari, which my father did not understand. After much searching, he found the home of Mer Akbar on a slope of the mountain Dihmazang.

My father looked for work in Kabul, but Mer Akbar encouraged him to attend one of the city's military schools, which provided free room and board and small salary. My father soon enrolled at a school called Harabi Shunzai (Army School).

Nine months later, my grandfather came to visit. When he learned from Mer Akbar that his son was attending school, he got very upset. At that time, Russia exerted influence over the Afghan government, and Pashtuns in the rural villages believed that people in Kabul wanted to spread communism and secular education throughout the territories. "Do you want my son to become kafer," my grandfather asked Mer Akbar; the word means non-Muslim. "Do you want him to forget his culture and religion?"

Mer Akbar tried to assure my grandfather that the school had no such intentions, but he was not satisfied and left the house, intending to take his son back to the village. But he too did not speak Dari, and while he struggled to find Harabi

Shunzai, Mer Akbar beat him there. He explained the situation to the principal and some teachers and asked them to help persuade my grandfather to let my father stay.

When he finally found the school, my grandfather had to wait for classes to end, and this made him even angrier. When my father approached him, my grandfather didn't recognize him at first because of his new clothes. Then he hugged and kissed his son. Then he slapped his face and said, "You must immediately change your clothes, and let us go."

"Okay, we will go home," my father said calmly, "but now it is time for praying. Let us go to the mosque and pray there."

After the prayers, the principal and teachers showed my grandfather around and explained what his son studied there. They assured him that the children prayed five times per day. They showed him the list of religious classes. They explained that his son wanted to become a police officer and help other people.

Amer Khan slowly came around. He spent more time there, sharing tea and dried fruit with his son. He admitted that he liked the friendly environment and religious devotion. Finally, he decided to let his son stay one more year. He cried when he left.

My father stayed at that school for ten years. After

earning a degree, he visited his family in the village. They told him it was time for him to marry, and that they'd already found him a wife, Sakeena. After the wedding, they moved to Kabul, where my father would work as a police officer. He built a house, and that's where they were living when I was born in 1986.

Chapter 1

My fondest memories of growing up in Kabul involve television and toilets. In the late 1980s the mujahideen, fighters with non-Muslim people, were still fighting the Soviet occupiers, but we were relatively safe in the neighborhood where my father had built our small house. Our neighbors had a black-and-white TV, and we were always welcome to watch with them. On Friday nights, the one station they could receive broadcast American or Indian movies, and this was the highlight of the week for my sister Sima and me. We would pray all week that the electricity would be working, and that our father would not make us help him clean the toilet.

Bathrooms in Afghanistan at the time used traditional dry-vault toilet systems. These need to be shoveled, and people usually did this at night. My father often chose Friday nights. He was a military man who didn't like anything that distracted us from our education, and he preferred that we spend the evening holding lights for him while he shoveled waste into a wheelbarrow. We would count the minutes, and often, by the time he released us, the movies were ending. But when we made it, or when father skipped the shoveling, it was pure joy. Our neighbors would greet us with dried fruit and tea and we all would lose ourselves in stories of people and places we could barely imagine.

It didn't last. After the Soviets left in 1989, Afghanistan was plunged into a civil war between the mujahideen rebels and the communist government. Even in Kabul, explosions became commonplace. Schools closed and electricity shut down all together. We stopped going to our neighbors' house; there were no movies on TV anyway. Some of our neighbors lost their jobs, some lost relatives. Food got scarce and the price of everything soared. I saw dead and injured people right in our neighborhood.

People started to move from the city to safer places. To protect me, their only son, my parents sent me to live with my grandparents and my uncle in Mangal, the village my father had left years before. This was in 1993. I was seven years old.

When it was time for me to leave, my mother and sister tried to prepare me for the trip and for life in my grandmother's house. "You must respect your grandmother and uncle's family, and not do anything that will make them upset with you," my mother told me. "We will come to you soon."

"What about school?" I asked. This worried me. I was in the first grade and did not want to leave my classmates.

"You will live in the village temporarily," my mother said. "Soon, the war situation in the city will get better, and you will come back. Until that time, you should focus on self-studying." She packed books and notebooks for me.

"Mom, please come soon to the village also. There is no food left at home. What are you going to eat?" This was my real fear.

"Do not worry, son," she replied. "God will help us. Your protection and safety are more important for us than food at this moment. In the village, you will not hear any sounds of bombs because Mangal is a very safe place."

When it was time to leave, everyone kissed and hugged me and offered more advice. I listened, but my mother's tears made me very weak and nervous. Finally, my grandmother took me with her back to Mangal, a place I'd never seen.

My grandmother, Aisha, lived with my uncle Dawood, his wife Fatima and their three daughters. Her house was very big, but only half of it was for people. The other half was for domestic animals and birds. That was my first time seeing farm animals. The day after I arrived, my grandmother taught me how to feed them. I became obsessed with the animals, and eventually took over the responsibility to feed and care for them.

Life in the village, however, was hard. The other boys did not speak Dari, and I did not speak their language, Pashto. I wore my city clothes; they wore traditional garb and hats. I was not familiar with their traditions and did not understand that wearing a hat is a sign of respect. Many of the villagers made fun of me, especially my accent and my clothes.

Over time even taking care of the animals felt like a burden. I missed my family. I missed the good times I'd had in Kabul with my friends and neighbors, watching movies and going to the zoo. I missed school. My parents had always told me I could be a doctor someday, and I wanted to surprise them by continuing my studies in the village. But Dawood and my grandmother would not send me. They wanted me to help with the animals. Dawood scoffed at the idea that I would be a doctor. We are farmers, he said; we raise animals and work in the fields. That was how I spent the last three months of first grade. Every morning I woke up, ate a slice of bread with the green tea, and pastured the animals in the fields until evening. When I went back, I ate bread, potatoes, and had a glass of milk, and helped my uncle in the fields.

One afternoon in the fields with the sheep and goats, while I was thinking about my family and hoping for the war to end, I noticed a man walking toward me. He wore a big hat, a long beard and a heavy old coat. As he got closer I saw him carrying a gun over his shoulder. "Hey, Turab Khan's son!" he called. "I got a letter from your father, and your father said that you should go to school. I am Uncle Shar Khan. Take your sheep home or ask somebody else to do it for you. Then, we will go to school."

I had heard of Uncle Shar Khan. I had been told he was very strong and brave. This man could be him, I thought, but I couldn't be sure. I also worried that if I went with him, Uncle Dawood would be angry. "I am sorry," I said, "but I cannot leave my animals here. My uncle will beat me, and my grandmother will be so mad at me. Or you might steal my sheep."

He laughed. "Kabuli guy, I am your uncle," he said. "Come here and give me a hug." I looked into his green eyes. His skin was white and his face was covered by a gray scraggly beard. I got close to him, and I hugged him. He kissed me on the cheek. I started to trust him —nobody had hugged me like this before.

"You are my brave, strong nephew. Is there anyone at home to take care of your animals, so I can take you to school? Go home, and ask somebody to come here."

"You might be my Uncle Shar Khan," I said. "Please could you go to my grandmother and ask her to come here and take care of the animals? Then I can go to school with you."

Further in the fields, there was a woman walking with a stick. Uncle Shar Khan said, "I think this is your grandmother.

We do not have to go to your house. She must take care of your animals today." He called her, "Heeeeyyy, Aisha!" She heard him, and started walking toward us.

Uncle Shar Khan laughed when she reached us. "Aisha, you will never die. Can you take care of these sheep, please? Your Kabuli boy does not know me, and he does not trust me enough to leave his animals."

My grandmother said, "Yes, he is city boy. What do you expect from him? He will learn our village way of life here."

"I am here to take him to school," Uncle Shar Khan told her. "If his father knows that he is not in school, then God bless us. He will be so upset. You know that he is a military officer. My nephew looks smart. He will be a big doctor someday." Uncle Shar Khan smiled at me when he said this.

My grandmother looked unhappy, but she relented. Uncle Shar Khan gave me his hand, and we left. I said, "God be with you, good bye, Grandmother." She grunted, "Come back soon!"

As we walked, Uncle Shar Khan told me stories about growing up in the village, but I could not pay attention. I was more interested in the gun slung over his shoulder and the pistol tucked inside his jacket. I tried to ask him why he needed these weapons, but he did not answer. He talked about school.

"I want to make my parents surprised and happy when I go back home," I said. "Can I become a doctor at this school?" He smiled and put his hand on my shoulder. He said, "Yes, you can become a doctor at this school, and your parents will be so proud of you."

There was a fast river between my uncle's Dawood house and the school, and the only very narrow bridge was made from wood that people had cut down and tied together. There was no railing. When I saw it my heart started racing and I told Uncle Shar Khan, "I am not going to this school." Uncle Shar Khan told me to be a strong man. He gave me his hand, and we walked through the bridge to the other side. I was relieved, but also worried about crossing it twice every day. I tried to think instead about the school, which I imagined being like the one I attended in Kabul, in a big modern building with nice tables and chairs.

We came upon groups of people in front of a black writing board. Some of them sat, some ran around, some were pushing each other and playing. Most of them were young, but there were two men with big hats and sticks in their hands, yelling at and hitting the boys. "What are these people doing?" I asked Uncle Shar Khan. "Who are they?"

He smiled and said, "That is your school."

Some of them noticed us — noticed me. They stared at

me and I could hear them talking about me. "Who is this guy? He looks very disco, probably from the city. We will show him the city."

One of the men with sticks called to Uncle Shar Khan and approached us. I would learn later that he was the principal of this school, but all I could think at that moment was that he looked nothing like my teachers in Kabul. The man hugged Uncle Shar Khan, then pointed at me with this huge stick. "Where did you get him from?" he asked my uncle, while looking at me. "He does not look like he belongs to your family."

"He is my strong nephew from Kabul. He should start school here. You should take care of him because his father took care of me. We are best friends and best cousins."

"Kabuli guy, where is your hat?" the man asked me. "You should have villager clothes. Do you speak Pashto?"

"If someone talks to me, I can understand," I replied. "I can speak also, but some phrases have mixed language."

"Okay," he said, "you can come to your school with your hat, and learn how to speak Pashto." He pointed at me with his stick again. "Let us go, I will take you to the class."

We walked to one of the groups of students of mixed age. Most of them were older than me. They were beating each other and saying bad words to each other. The principal told me to go sit. Then he said to the class, "This is a new student."

The others stared at me. Some asked questions. "Hey, which village are you from? What are you doing here?" Some of the kids touched my pants to feel the unfamiliar material. I was so foreign to them. "You are a Persian guy. Do you know how to pray? Do you know how to speak?" In my broken Pashto, I replied, "My name is Atal. I came from Kabul city."

We studied just one subject in a day. There were three teachers in the whole school. When they were busy with their fields and animals, or when the weather was bad, we did not have class.

Other children bullied me because of my language. When they made fun of me, the teacher joined in. After school, students tried to beat me up. They wanted to fight with me every day. Along with this, crossing the river every day was still a huge problem for me. Sometimes the water level rose high enough that it touched the wooden bridge. The water ran very fast, and I did not know how to swim. I started skipping school. There was no point, I wasn't really learning anything. My uncle thought that I was going to school every day, but some days I just sat near the river instead.

There was one boy who was friendly. His name was Ismail, and we became friends. He was always asking about my life in Kabul. He told me that he came to the school just to hear my stories about the animals in the Kabul Zoo and TV shows that I had seen. I liked to tell him stories because they reminded me of the happy times I had in Kabul. I enjoyed Ismail's company and attention. He asked me to tell him the same stories many times, and he was very curious about all the details I could offer about the zoo and the movies. He dreamed about just seeing and touching a TV or going to Kabul City to see the zoo. He asked so many questions. "What is the electricity? How does TV work?" He would walk with me to the bridge if I told him stories, and I would try not to finish until we got there, so he wouldn't leave.

It was hard for me to tell him the stories sometimes because I was still learning his language. He was trying to learn Dari, too. The other students hated us and fought with us because of this. Ismail walked to school from a different village, but sometimes he helped me to walk across the bridge by standing on one side and calling out to me, "Go, Atal! I am watching. If something happens to you, I'll call for help!"

Back at home, my uncle and grandmother's attitudes toward me began to change. They felt that I did not help them enough. My grandmother complained about this everyday. They saved work for me to do when I got back from school. One day, my grandmother probed, "You are going to school, but we have never seen any books or ink on your hands." By this time, I had just one torn notebook with one pencil.

One night, Dawood and my grandmother asked me what my teacher's name was. I could not reply because I did not know. They told me, "You are going to school, but have you learned how to pray and read religious books?"

"I have not seen any of my teachers," I admitted. "Sometimes they come, but it is too crowded to hear their words. They just talk about village life. Most of the students do not have any books. I do not understand my teachers because they speak Pashto. It is hard for me to understand what they are talking about. When they ask me questions, I cannot give them answers. Other students make fun of me, and they laugh. I get so nervous and embarrassed. When the classes are over, the students want to fight me and beat me on my way back home. They tell their dogs to run after me and bite me. Every day in class, I worry about what is going to happen when I leave. Now, I have villager clothes and a hat, but still my language is not good. They do not like me."

I also told them about Ismail. I thought they would be glad that I made a friend, but their point of view was different. They scolded, "You go there to talk about Kabul City and movies? You do not know your teachers' names?"

"I go there because Uncle Shar Khan told me I could

become a doctor to surprise my parents," I said. "My father will get angry at me and beat me if I do not go to school. I am afraid of his reaction."

My Aunt Fatima was there during this conversation, and she told grandmother and Dawood, "What the boy is telling you is true. I did not tell you, but dogs have really chased him, and he has been beaten by the boys at school."

They decided it was better that I did not go to the school anymore. "Instead of wasting time at school, you can help us. You will take care of the animals again every day. We will give you better food now." After that conversation, I did not go to that school, and I did not see Ismail anymore. I missed him. I had told him part of a story and was supposed to finish it next time I saw him.

The only reminder I had of Ismail was a gift he had given me, a toy pistol with wooden bullets. He said that I should use it for my protection. The pistol made me feel brave and powerful. I always kept it with me. But I knew that it was not a real pistol like Uncle Shar Khan had. I hoped that one day I would be able to get his real pistol.

No longer a student, I started to get more involved in village life and became interested in villagers' beliefs. I continued to help my uncle with the animals and the fields.

Often I carried a shovel. My uncle would have me dig a trench to reroute a mountain stream so that it would irrigate the crops.

Sometimes, when a baby boy was born in somebody's house, my uncles and I went to congratulate the families. Both men and women went. The men wore their new turbans for this occasion. They carried their guns, and, as was the tradition, they shot bullets into the air to celebrate. Very often, my uncles Dawood and Shar Khan put one of their guns into my hands, and they steadied it with one hand to help me hold the gun. They told me when to pull the trigger. Bang! When I took a shot, the gun jumped and pushed hard into my chest. The sound was very loud, and to be honest, I was so afraid I nearly cried.

"You must not cry," my uncles remarked. "You are our nephew. Be a strong man. Don't embarrass us by crying and being afraid of guns in front of our people. You should learn to be a brave person."

This happened often enough that I started to enjoy shooting a gun into the air and wanted to do it more and more.

Uncle Shar Khan and I grew closer. To make me happy, he often gave me hard candy or dried apricots. I always asked to play with the pistol that he carried everywhere for protection (someone from the village had threatened to kill him.) I asked him if he could buy a pistol for me. Uncle said I would get his pistol when I grew into adulthood.

I started measuring my height and foot size daily. I checked my mustache in the mirror. I carried a big shovel to show him that I was a big man already.

He usually came to our house around sunset. When my uncle arrived, I always ran to the front door to give him a hug and get his pistol to play with. He allowed me to have it, but he always took the bullets out of the pistol first. I was so happy that I had a new friend because I still missed Ismail a lot.

Sometimes I tried to shepherd the animals close to his house just so I could see him. When he saw me, and he would call out, "Come here, my brave nephew!" and I would leave the animals and run to him. He gave me green tea with bread, and he told me stories. After a while, Uncle Shar Khan would remind me not to leave the sheep too long because they might run into other villagers' fields and destroy them. He warned that the villagers would get very upset with me.

Uncle taught me many things. He taught me about the *shaftala*, or clover that we grew in our fields in summer and harvested and dried in autumn for feed in winter. He taught me that even though the sheep loved the clover, only so much could be given because excess caused bloat.

One day I left the animals and stayed with Uncle Shar Khan for a little longer than usual. While I was with him, the animals roamed into a neighbor's field. When I got back, I discovered that one white sheep had eaten too much shaftala grass. I took the other sheep home, but I left the sick one behind because it could not walk.

I ran home wondering what would happen to my white sheep. I told my grandmother, "The white sheep is in the field. It is very sick." As we hurried to the sheep, my grandmother repeatedly slapped me on the back of my neck, telling me, "Your uncle will kill you!"

We reached the poor sickened white sheep still alive but unable to walk. Its stomach had grown enormous from bloat. We called a villager who was working in the fields nearby and asked him for help. He saw the sheep, ran to his house and returned with a big knife. He said, "This sheep will not survive. We must kill it." He put the big blade under the sheep's head and sliced its neck. The red blood gushed everywhere. He held the poor sheep until all the blood had left its body.

I began to cry for my little white sheep. I remembered about my uncle — he was going to be furious! The villager began to tell my grandmother that he always saw me leaving my sheep and running to Uncle Shar Khan's fields to spend time with him. He said he saw me sitting with Uncle Shar Khan there and not paying attention to the sheep. Grandmother beat me after this right then and there in the field. I felt so bad about what I had done that the beating was justified.

Several villagers helped carry the dead sheep back to the property. My Uncle Dawood returned from the fields and came through the gate just after. He was told that the sheep died because I was with Uncle Shar Khan. Then, the owner of the shaftala field came to our house. When he saw me he said, "Your nephew left his sheep unattended, and they destroyed my field. They trampled everything!"

He looked directly at me, and he warned, "If I catch your sheep in my field again, I will beat you so badly." I was so ashamed that I couldn't respond.

After he left, Dawood slapped me across my face and kicked me again and again. He told me I was not allowed to meet with Uncle Shar Khan or go to his house anymore. I cried the whole night.

The next day, I woke up with a fever. Uncle Dawood's sister, my Aunt Sharifa, was at our house. She lived six villages away from our village. She saw me, and she said, "Do not worry about the sheep." She yelled at my uncle, "He is a small child. Everybody makes mistakes." She said that she would take me to her house for a couple of nights. I was relieved and even a little excited, but I still wanted to see Uncle Shar Khan.

When Uncle Dawood came on his tractor two days later to take me home, he repeated that I was not to see Uncle Shar Khan anymore. "Do you know who Uncle Shar Khan is?" he asked.

"Yes, he is my uncle, and he is my friend," I said.

"Some people are looking for him to kill him," my uncle said. "If you are with him, they will kill you, too."

I got surprised. Immediately I wanted to find out why those people wanted to kill him. I was also a little upset that Uncle Shar Khan had not shared this information with me. He always told me stories, but he did not tell me anything about himself.

My uncle lifted me up onto the shelf at the back of the tractor. He started the engine and off we went toward home. I could feel every bump on the way. When he crossed the river, I shut my eyes and prayed we would cross safely.

I felt relieved when he pulled in through the big gates and helped me off the tractor. It was afternoon by then, and I ran to the sheep to take them to pasture. Standing at the door, my grandmother pointing her index finger at me. "Welcome back," she said. "You are not to to meet with Uncle Shar Khan or you kill more sheep. Villagers will complain that our sheep go to their fields and eat their corn and wheat. Do you want to create trouble for your Uncle Dawood? I do not want him to have to argue and fight with our village neighbors because of you."

Trying to assure her, I said "Grandmother, I will not leave them again. Everything will be okay. Calm down." She glared at me. I hurried out.

I did not plan to leave the sheep, but I decided to take them a little closer to Uncle Shar Khan's house.

I sat with the sheep, and I kept staring at his house from the hillside. I longed to see him. All I could see was his property. There were several family houses. A mosque stood nearby. There was a big tree that villagers said was at least three hundred years old. I still did not see him, but there were a lot of other people walking around his house. Uncle Shar Khan was never in sight. I waited until the sun set behind the mountain. Everything got dark, and the birds stopped singing. The village was totally empty. It was so dark that I was not able to see his door. The sheep stopped eating. I sat in the middle of them feeling so sad. Feeling dejected, I took the sheep back to the house. When I reached the door, my grandmother started yelling at me because she said I was late. She checked all the sheep, and she was happy that the sheep were so full. Sheep that ate a lot always made my grandmother happy. I went to my bed without dinner. It was not really a bed as I had known in Kabul. It was a very old cushion made with cotton. I fell asleep thinking about Uncle Shar Khan.

Chapter 2

The next morning, I took my toy pistol with me when I took the sheep out. Again I watched Uncle Shar Khan's house and fields that were about four hundred feet away from me, but still I did not see him. Maybe his enemies had caught him, I thought. Around mid-morning, I saw several groups of people arrive at his guest house. They wore turbans with long, flowing, white and brown scarves over their long dress-like Sharts and baggy pants. Most of them looked old. Each carried some type of gun.

As I watched, I got more and more confused. At first I thought he was not coming out because of the people Uncle Dawood warned me about. Then I thought that maybe Uncle Shar Khan died. But no one looked like they were coming to a funeral. They did not look unhappy.

Several young men brought trays of tea pots and short glasses to the old tree where the important men had gathered. His family members walked back and forth to serve the guests. They did not seem sad. So what could the cause of this gathering be, I wondered. Perhaps Uncle Shar Khan's wife had given birth to a baby boy (the birth of a girl would not have been cause for visits and congratulations; it was considered a disappointment in Mangal). Or perhaps his brother had gotten married, or someone had gotten engaged. But by then I had learned enough about village life to know that if this were a celebration, bullets would be flying into the sky.

I decided I had to get close to his house and figure out what was going on there, but I could not leave my sheep. Close by, five young boys were watching their sheep. They were not usually nice to me, but I was getting desperate. I led my sheep near, so they could hear me say hello to them. They teased, "Hey, Kabuli boy. What are you doing here? How come you decided to come by us? We might need to beat you a little bit."

They started asking me to pronounce different words in Pashto. I answered as well as I could. Each time I made a mistake they slapped me. I was focused on finding someone to watch my sheep for a little bit, so I put up with their teasing. I wanted to run to Uncle Shar Khan's house for a couple of minutes, and I was willing to do whatever it took to get the boys to help me.

They tried to get rid of me, but I begged them to allow me to stay longer. One replied, "You are not one of us. You came from a different city. You do not know our language."

Another chimed in, "Look at your clothes. We are embarrassed by you. Go back to your field. Do not stay here with us."

"Please, please, please," I begged, "look after my sheep

for a short time."

Then I remembered the wooden pistol. It was a very unusual thing in the village because children did not have any toys. "Boys, look at my pistol," I said. "Let us play with it."

All five boys surrounded me. They tried to take the pistol away from me, but I told them that the pistol would stay in my hand. I did not trust them. I asked them if they knew what was happening at my Uncle Shar Khan's house. They started laughing, and they said, "Isn't he your friend? You should know what is going on in his house. Maybe his wife or his daughter died. You are always with him. He had to tell you what is going on in his house."

I pleaded, "Please, keep an eye on my sheep. I will be back very fast."

They did not want to do it. They said, "Your sheep die too fast. We do not want to be in a trouble."

"If you take care of my animals now, I will bring some candy from my home tomorrow, and we will shoot bullets from my pistol."

"We do not trust you," one said. "If you see your Uncle Shar Khan, you will forget about us and forget to give us the sweets tomorrow."

One of the older boys, a leader of the group, offered, "I will take care of your sheep, but you should give me your

36

pistol."

"Okay, I will go, and when I come back, I will give you the pistol to play with."

"No," he said, "you should give the pistol to me now, and then it's mine. You cannot take it back from me."

"I cannot. It is a gift from my friend. I keep it for protection. If wolves attack my sheep, I will have the gun to protect them."

They started arguing with me and pushed me. I said, "Wait! Wait! Okay! I will give it to you." I wanted to see Uncle Shar Khan, and I thought seeing him was above all else. I asked, "Do you really promise to take care of my sheep?"

"If you give us the pistol with all the wooden bullets, we will take care of your sheep," said the leader.

I quickly pulled the pistol and the bullets out of my pocket. I set them in front of the boys. "Take it."

After they grabbed it, they checked my pockets to see if there were any bullets left. I had given them everything. They said, "Now you are free to go, but do not stay with your Uncle Shar Khan too long."

"I will go for a little while," I assured them. "Do not tell my grandmother and uncle about this."

"We will not tell them anything if you bring us candy tomorrow. The pistol is just the price for going to Uncle Shar

Khan but not for keeping it a secret from your grandmother and uncle."

I promised to bring them candy, then ran to Uncle Shar Khan's house as fast as my feet would take me, glancing back to make sure grandmother was not watching. I crossed road through the valley to his house. There were dogs in the fields. I was frightened of these dogs. I dodged the dogs chained to the house next to his.

After what seemed like forever, I made it to Uncle Shar Khan's house. There were a lot of people coming in and out of the house. I looked at the people by the big tree. It was where young men usually gathered in the evening and spent time together. I stopped there first. It was afternoon. I saw some young boys. They carried food and bread pasti wrapped in long woolen towels, which they unfolded in front of the seated guest. Others brought pots full of stew.

I stood close to the tree. Children did not notice me because they were playing together. I waited to see Uncle Shar Khan. I saw people that were coming in and out with different food. People were not done eating, so I decided to stay longer.

The guest house was full of people, but there was no sign of Uncle Shar Khan. I wanted to see his face and convince myself that he was still alive. I saw that people were not sad, but his absence confused me. I tried to listen to the people's conversations, but they spoke in Pashto and it was hard for me to understand. Uncle Dawood would be inside, so I could not go in.

Finally, people started to come out of the house. Young boys were standing with water and towels. They were pouring water on guests' hands after they finished their meals, preparing to have green tea. I still waited, and the time moved very slowly. Drinking tea took more time. There were two sheep that were tied next to the tree. I felt bad for the sheep because they did not have any grass, so I tried giving them some. Someone shouted for me to leave them alone because they would be slaughtered soon.

I went a little further and sat on the edge of the field. Three older people came out of the guest house, whispering to each other. After some discussion, they returned to the house. After a while these three people left the house again and continued talking.

I was getting very hungry and tired. To keep myself busy, I was sitting at the edge of a stream nearby, skipping stones across the water. Suddenly I heard shooting. I was so afraid thinking that it might be fighting, but then I saw that it was the people at my uncle's house, firing into the air. They looked happy and excited and said congratulations to each other.

The rest of the people came out from the *hojra*, guest house. They were laughing, but still Uncle Shar Khan was not there. Two people came for the sheep and pushed them through the crowd of people in front of the guest house. Then they slaughtered the sheep.

Young men carried baskets full of the chocolates and sweets, and they offered them to everyone. I stayed away, still afraid that Uncle Dawood would see me. Finally, I heard the voice of Uncle Shar Khan, who was approaching the crowd. My heart started pounding, but the discomfort and weakness from lack of food faded. I was thrilled that Uncle Shar Khan was still alive! I got a little closer. He had a wide smile on his face. His clothes were white, but his coat was the same old one he always wore. He strode into the middle of the crowd, talking loudly and greeting them.

I was so happy and wanted to join the celebration. I ran to the man with the basket of chocolates and grabbed two handfuls. I wanted to greet Uncle Shar Khan, but because I saw Uncle Dawood next to him, I did not say anything. I decided to go back to my sheep.

Grinning from ear to ear, I ran back. The sheep were further from where I had left them, and the boys were farther still. When they saw me they called, "Heeey, Persian boy, come here!"

When I got close I saw that they were playing with the pistol. One of them pointed the pistol at me and said, "We will shoot you with your pistol if you spend so much time there again or if your sheep go to our fields!"

"You said you were going to be there for a short time," another complained, "but you spent hours there!"

The boys saw my pockets full of chocolates, and they took almost all of them. I was still so happy that Uncle Shar Khan was alive that I did not stop them.

But I still could not figure out what was going on there. When I got home I asked my grandmother.

"Stop!" she commanded. "Shut up your mouth! You are asking too many questions. Go eat and sleep. It is not for small kids."

"Please, tell me a little bit," I begged. I took what was left of the chocolate from pockets. "Where did you get these chocolates?" my grandmother demanded. "Dawood brought the same chocolates from the party today. Did you go to his house again? Did you leave your sheep?"

"Villager kids helped me!" I said. "Please, do not tell anything to uncle. I saved chocolates for you. I just wanted to see Uncle Shar Khan because I thought somebody killed him!"

"You are crazy," she replied. "Did not you realize that

nobody died in the village? If somebody dies in our family, you will not understand, will you? Get out from here, silly and crazy guy!"

"Come on, Grandmother, please tell me the story about Uncle Shar Khan!"

"Tomorrow. We have guests tonight. Get out now."

The next day, it was all I could think about. At the end of the day, I took my sheep home as early in the evening as possible. But the guests were still in our house. They were nice people, but I was not happy to see them because it meant my grandmother would again refuse to tell me the story.

I asked my Aunt Fatima who they were.

"The guests came from your Aunt Nazira's house.," she explained. "They are preparing a wedding party, and they want to discuss it with your uncle. They also have to resolve some disagreements between our families. Your Uncle Dawood invited them to come here and talk about the problems."

"What is the disagreement?"

"It is about your Aunt Nazira's daughter, your cousin Gulana, who is lame. She is getting married. The other girl will be joining your family instead of Gulana. The argument is about switching these girls between the families."

"Oh my God, how will my cousin marry if she cannot walk?" I asked. I was suddenly worried about her. "Gulana will not be able to handle housework in the village."

My aunt promised to tell me everything later, and she went to cook dinner.

After we gave them dinner, I was walking back and forth from my house to my uncle's *hojra*, taking the food to the people. I was getting tired because these two locations were a little far from each other. After the dinner, the guests and my family got angry and started screaming. It was hard to understand. I heard one of the guests tell Nazira's husband, "Your daughter cannot walk properly. She is disabled."

"On the other hand," Nazira's husband said, "Your daughter is crazy and so withdrawn." That was all I could make out. It was almost midnight, so I went to my grandmother, but she was not in the mood to tell me the story. Before I went to bed, my uncle told me, "Be at home early tomorrow. We will not be at home because Uncle Shar Khan has invited me to his house in the evening. You will stay at home. I might stay at his house for the night because it is not safe to walk in the village at night."

The next day I came back from the fields with a big smile on my face — I was eager to hear what had happened at Uncle Shar Khan's house. Unfortunately, on that night my grandmother had a slight fever and was coughing. I did everything she asked in order to keep her happy, but she still was not in any mood to tell me the story. The house was quiet. My aunt with her three daughters cooked dinner. My uncle was not at home. I came to sit close to my grandmother. We had dinner, but I didn't have much appetite.

I was looking at her eyes and was trying to understand her mood because she usually was not very nice to me. The nicest thing that she had ever done for me was not telling my uncle that I had left the sheep and gone to Uncle Shar Khan's. I wanted to ask her again to tell me the story, but I was afraid that she might smack me in my face or yell at me. She finished her food and told me to bring her jainamaz, her prayer rug, so she could pray. I wanted to do her this favor, but my cousin Leila reached the prayer rug before me, lay it on the floor, and pointed it in the direction of Mecca. I had missed a chance to get in her good graces.

After praying for a long time, my grandmother called to my aunt, "Fatima, can you prepare my bed to sleep?"

With these words, I became so sad. I lost all my energy. I asked her one more time to tell me the story, but she started to yell and ordered me to bring her medication. Still hopeful, I quickly obeyed and went into her room. But there was no light so I was slow in returning and she got annoyed again.

Aunt Fatima asked, "Can you help me with the cows? I

44

must milk them. You can hold the lamp." With lanterns in hand, Leila and I followed my aunt. My aunt began to milk the cows.

The lamp was shining brightly on my face. She looked at me and asked, "What happened? Why do you look so sad?"

"Grandmother promised to tell me what happened at Uncle Shar Khan's house a few days ago, but she did not. She wouldn't tell me anything."

"I know the story myself. I will tell you."

"Do you really know about it!, Aunt!?" I was so excited.

"Yes," she replied. "But first, tell me about your visit at your mother's cousin Majeed's house last week. You saw Majeed's new wife? Tell me about her. What is she like?"

"Her name is Zarina," I answered. I pointed to Leila and continued, "Zarina is the same age as Leila. Fourteen. They look almost alike. Aunt, is it possible to marry a very young child with an old man?"

"It might happen." Sadness came to her face, and tears appeared in her eyes. "Tell me more about Zarina," she asked. So I began to tell the story of how we met.

Chapter 3

Uncle Dawood had sent me to Majeed's home to fetch the sharpening stone for the scythe. I went to the front gate and knocked on the door. A dog started barking very loudly. However, nobody came to open the gate. I knocked on the door again and again with a stone. I was about to leave, but through the gap of the big wooden gates, I noticed a girl completely covered in a bright green and red chador. Her cover was spotted with dirt. She was just standing there. That was strange to me. Why wasn't she opening the door? Maybe someone was playing a joke on me. I called to her. She came closer to the door but still she did not make any attempt to open it.

"Who is this?" she asked.

Thinking it was one of my cousins, I said, "Are you playing a joke? I am Atal! You know me."

"I do not know you," she said. She sounded afraid.

"This is Atal. From Kabul."

"Oh, Kabuli boy! Your uncle told me about you. Come inside." She opened the gate and offered her hand covered by her scarf. It was shaking. Her face was totally covered. She said, "Let us go inside."

"Uncle Dawood has sent me here to fetch the sharpening stone," I explained. "Where are my aunt, my Uncle

Majeed, and the family?'

"I am Zarina. I am your uncle Majeed's new wife. All the family has gone to a wedding party two villages away."

The dog was still barking at me. It was chained to a big wooden stake in the ground, but I was afraid to walk through the yard. Zarina tried to assure me, "Do not worry. It will not bite you. Give me your hand. Let us go inside." We passed by the dog and went in. All I could think about was how I would get past that dangerous animal when it was time to leave.

"I have to get the stone and return to my uncle's," I said.

"You cannot go now," she replied. "You must have tea and something to eat. You are so cute, Kabuli boy. I will not let you go. Your uncles will be so mad at me if I do not feed you and give you some tea. I will cook you some eggs and potatoes, a usual village dish." I was elated! I loved potatoes and eggs. And I was happy to neglect my duty of watching the sheep for as long as I could.

When my Aunt Fatima heard that I had stayed at Zarina's house to eat, she looked mortified. "Why did you stay there for food?"

"I was really afraid of the dog, Aunt."

"Okay, tell me more. What was she like? Tell me more

about her."

"She was great, Aunt. After Zarina and I came inside of the room, she told me to sit. She ran to the yard to prepare tea. I was very surprised because she did not uncover her face in front of me. I was just a little boy, yet she kept her face completely covered the whole time I was there."

"Silly city boy," Aunt Fatima said. "Zarina is a new bride. She must not show her face in front of anyone for years. What happened next?"

I noticed two windows across from me. I was able to see a huge backyard. There were some cows among a small herd of sheep and chickens. Then I saw Zarina. She was taking a big metal pot blackened from fire to the well to fill it with water. It took her some time. As I watched through the window, I could see the bucket was heavy for her. I felt so bad for her. I feared that she might fall down the well. I felt guilty that I had created such a hardship. I stood up to go out until I remembered the dog. Zarina finally pulled up the water bucket, poured it into the black pot, and brought it inside to boil the water on the burner of the wooden stove. Everything that she was doing was a hardship for her. After she finished, she ran back to me.

"I am sorry it is taking so long to prepare the tea," she said. "It will be ready soon. I like your name, Atal, but can I call you 'City guy' or 'Kabuli boy?'"

"Yes, you can. Can I call you my aunt then?' I was not able to see her face, but I felt that she smiled.

"It is good enough, but I would prefer that you call me Zarina."

"My family will be mad at me if I call you by name. It is very disrespectful."

"I will not tell anyone that you call me Zarina."

"I'm sorry. I can't. I can call you my little aunt."

She was amused. "Fine. I hope you aren't getting bored waiting for the tea." She went to a different room and brought back an album of family pictures. "Look at this album," she said, placing it on my lap. "You can ask me about who the people in the pictures are when I return with the tea."

From the windows, I saw her again running back and forth. She went to the cows, checked the tea pot, and gathered some eggs and potatoes. She tried to prepare food very fast, but she had a lot of other work around the house, too. As soon as she completed one task, another one was always waiting for her. Finally, the water for the tea began to boil. She took the tea pot with her scarf, and poured the hot water into a small pot with green tea. Then she brought it into the room where I was waiting. I pretended to be busy with the pictures.

She brought the tea with some sweets and apologized,

"I am sorry that you had to wait so long. I am still not done with my housework. You can continue looking at the pictures while you are drinking your tea."

There were not many pictures, so I looked at each several times. In the middle of the album, I found an envelope among the photos. Thinking it might have some photos inside, I opened it, and I found a letter written in pencil. I put the letter back and sipped some tea. Each time my cup was nearly empty, she'd return and refill it and bring more sweets and apologize again for being so busy.

When the sweets were gone, I decided to go outside and help her because I was sorry for her. I carried the pictures out to the yard with me. She was standing in front of the tandoor oven. It was made of mud-brick with smooth clay on the inside. I was so surprised how she could bake pasti bread in such a deep tandoor. I could feel the heat from the wood deep inside the oven. She looked very nervous preparing the dough for the bread. I wondered how she would be able to bend down to reach inside the smoky oven to stick the bread to the walls of the tandoor. As she tried, some of it fell into the fire, causing the ashes to fly. She was too small to reach. As each bread turned a golden brown, she had to remove it from the hot oven. After she stacked the last of this batch of bread, I asked her to tell me about the photos.

She was working to make the fire a little hotter. She took a big metal hook to roll the wood to bring it back up to temperature and remove the smoke to bake the bread. The fire was not ready yet, so she covered the tandoor oven back with the cover. "Okay," she agreed. "Let us take the album, and I will tell you."

I took out a photo. "Who is this person?"

"This is my grandfather. He was a very brave person."

We went through the other photos. Finally, I asked about the letter.

She quickly snatched it from my hands. She kissed the letter, and she said, "How did you find it? I thought I had lost it!"

"Is it yours? Who is it from? Are you able to read it?" I was amazed when she said yes. So few people I knew could read.

She became exuberant. "This letter is from my best friend, Wagma. We lived in the same little village. We grew up together, played together, and shared secrets together." Suddenly, she stopped talking and her face changed. "I miss Wagma so very much. She was my dear friend."

"Why don't you go back to your house and visit her?" I asked. "She is not that far from you."

"No, I cannot meet her anymore. I will not be able to

see her. But it is my dream to see her one more time in my life. To make sure she is okay. But it is impossible. I am so worried about her!"

"Why is it impossible? What happened?"

I knew that she was crying, and I wanted to cheer her up. She was not much older than me. I felt so comfortable with her and wanted to play. I wanted to tease her a little, so I asked her to remove her scarf. I told her that because her face was covered it made more difficult to bake the bread and talk to me. I don't know how I was able to understand how miserable she was at my young age, but I needed to help her in some way. I said to her, "Please, remove the chador from your face. You will burn yourself or fall into the tandoor fire."

"Okay," she agreed, "but do not tell anyone that I showed my face to you. It will be disrespectful to them." I assured her I wouldn't.

Aunt Fatima looked at me and said, "You are such a bad boy! You promised not to tell anyone, yet you told me."

"Oh, I totally forgot! Aunt, please do not tell anyone."

"Silly boy!" she said, smiling. "Continue."

"I am so shy," Zarina said, "but I know you are a good little boy. You are like a little brother to me."

She took off her face cover. Her eyes were full of tears and her makeup was smeared under her eyes. She told me she was so shy she couldn't look at me. "I do not have a brother to come and ask me how I am here," she said. "I am happy that I can tell you my story."

As she wiped away her tears, I noticed that her hands were black from smoke and soil, and had many small cuts and abrasions.

"I will tell you a little about Wagma while we are waiting for the pesti," she said. "Let me begin by telling you how I learned to read."

As I was saying these words, I noticed Aunt Fatima's eyes were full of tears. I looked over at Leila still holding the lamp. Her eyes were full of tears, too. "Why are you crying?" I asked. "What is happening?"

"It might happen to my Leila," Aunt Fatima explained. "My husband wants a boy, so he is planning to take a second wife. He wants sons to help him in the fields and with the animals. A son will bring him more respect in the family and more status in the village. A son can help protect. Why am I crying? If my husband marries a second time and brings his new wife here, in return for his new wife, I will have to give my daughter to that family. We do not have enough money to pay a dowry. My daughter is only fifteen years old. She is not ready to run a household. I pray to Allah that the baby that I am pregnant with is a boy!"

Our whole family had been praying that Fatima would give Uncle Dawood the baby boy he had been longing for since they first married. Everybody was concerned because my aunt had lost several babies. In the village, we did not have basic medical care.

"Back to Zarina's story," she said. "Tell me." So I continued.

"When I was still living at my father's house," Zarina began, "Wagma and I used to walk to the valley for water all the time. My family and her family were friends. Neither of us had brothers. Her father worked very hard in the fields. Her father was very tired because there were no male family members to help him with all the farm chores.

"We grew up together. Wagma was the prettiest girl in the whole village. She was a very good girl, always kind and respectful, and she was smart. She knew how to read and write because her father was a very educated person and wanted her to be educated, too. Her father had studied in Kabul City. He lives in the village now. Wagma always encouraged me to study in her house. I told my parents, and my mother said that I could. I went to her house every day. We studied together. Both of her parents and her older sisters helped us. Her father asked a mullah from the local mosque to help the children in the village with their education by creating a school in his mosque. Much like Wagma's father, the mullah had come from Kabul when it had become dangerous. The mullah agreed and began to teach religious subjects at the mosque. Wagma and I were among his students at his school. After a short time, unfortunately, Wagma's mother became sick and became weaker and weaker every day.

"I enjoyed studying at the mosque and playing with Wagma and the other girls of my family in her house. I was happy there. Every morning, she and I and all the other village girls strolled to the valley to fetch water for our homes. But Wagma and I would sit off to the side and talk. Besides fetching water, Wagma also had to take care of the sheep. Sometimes her father had Wagma help him in the fields. They always went at nightfall so that nobody could see her outside during the day. As I told you, she was a strikingly beautiful girl. A lot of families were interested in her. Many came to her family's house to offer marriage proposals. But her parents were educated, and they rejected every single engagement proposition because they understood Wagma was much too young to get married yet. Wagma's father wanted the best for

Wagma and all his daughters. He hoped that one day they would be able to move back to Kabul and his daughters would be able to get a proper education.

"Wagma's uncles, on the other hand, advised her father not to reject a good marriage offer. They told him to use her to his advantage. It would be better for her father to find a second wife who might give him sons. They told him, 'It is important to have sons. You have a beautiful daughter. Every family wants your daughter for their sons. It is a good opportunity for you to build alliances and build your wealth. Take advantage of it!'

"Wagma's father always countered that sons were not more valuable than daughters, that he loved his three daughters, and that they were too young to marry.

"Day by day, her mother's ill health was taking its toll on poor Wagma. She did not smile much. She confided in me that her mother had cancer. She was so weak that she was unable to walk anymore. They had taken her to the local doctor, and he prescribed some medications. The doctor had told her father that due to the serious progression of the cancer, it was not possible to cure her in that hospital. He urged him to take her to Pakistan where there were better doctors, and her mother might have a very small chance to survive. But the doctor warned that staying in the hospital in Pakistan would certainly cost a great many Pakistani rupees.

"Their situation was dreadful by this time, so I stopped going to Wagma's house. They had enough problems to deal with. I still continued going to the mosque school for a little while, but my male cousins did not want me to go there. It was harmful for their family prestige to have a girl go out of the house to study. Finally, they stopped me from studying there. I was not permitted to attend school, and I was not able to play and study with Wagma anymore. In fact, I almost never saw her unless we met in the valley to get water. When we met, Wagma described her family's situation. Her father was desperately trying to find the money for the hospital stay. He knocked on the doors of all their relatives. Nobody wanted to help them. They knew there would be no hope to get that money back because there were no sons in that family to help his father earn that kind of money.

"With no other alternative, her father decided to sell their cow. It had always provided the milk for their table and for yogurt and butter. The cow was sold with her calf, so they managed to get quite a bit of money for it. Nonetheless, the doctor told them that what they had managed to collect was not enough. Next, her father sold his trees from his fields for lumber. He was still short. Finally, her father decided to reach out to one more family to whom he was related. There was no other way. The people in the Mirbaz family were not nice people, but they were rich. From all the various relatives, this was the only family that agreed to lend Wagma's father the money he needed.

"However, it was not without penalty. This family and his had been feuding for years over a dispute between Wagma's great-grandfather and great-grandfather Mirbaz. The agreement was that Wagma's father's fields would become the property of the Mirbaz family for one year and until the loan was paid back. They knew that Wagma's father would not be able to return the money. Their real interest was in one of his daughters as repayment for the borrowed money. But this was his only chance to save his precious wife, and he accepted it.

"He finally took his wife to Pakistan. Wagma and her sisters, of course, did not go with her but were left at home to tend to the farm. For one month, there was no communication from the parents. During this awful time while her mother and father were staying in Pakistan, I was always trying to make Wagma happy and distract her from her worries. My mother and I would visit to encourage her to stay strong and assure her that her mother would get well. The sisters asked us to stay in the house with them.

"Wagma and her sisters were hopeful. When someone knocked on the gate, they would hurry to check. Their dreams at night were about their mother returning. As the days turned into weeks, their food supply dwindled to almost nothing. There was only a little flour and a bit of corn. Unfortunately, the village dam came to their house, and they had to give what little food there was to him."

I interrupted to ask, "Who is dam, Zarina?"

She smiled. "Like in all villages, the dam is the person who takes care of the preparations for all the big events in life such as funerals, weddings and parties. His payment is in food. So when the dam came, they had to give him all that they could.

"One night at home, I heard the sound of a car near Wagma's house. My father and my uncles went to see what was happening. When they returned, my mother asked my father what had happened, and he told her that Wagma's mother had died in Pakistan, and her body had been brought to the village.

"Neighbors and the dam came to their house to prepare the body for burial. When I arrived, I saw Wagma. Her heart was broken because, until the last moment, she hoped that she would see her mother alive. Her family had lost everything. There was no more happiness for them. Now, her father got sick, too. Wagma was the one who had to take care of her father and the rest of the family. They worried about all the money they owed. There was no income to be made because they did not have fields to work.

"Soon the Mirbaz family started harassing Wagma's family. The fields were not very productive and they were not satisfied with what the crops yielded. They demanded full payment as soon as he could pay. Wagma's father asked them to keep the fields for one more year and extend the payment of the debt, but they were uncompromising. Her father's health worsened. After the given year, the situation became so critical that her father was not able to deal with the stress and pressure. He had a heart attack and died, leaving Wagma and her sisters all alone.

"By the decision of the village, Wagma and her younger sister were given to the Mirbaz family. Her sister was only eleven at the time, so only Wagma was married into the family. There was no wedding or negotiation for Wagma. This was a forced marriage and that meant her life was going to be very hard. Her uncle decided to protect the younger sister by making a marriage to his own son. But he worried that the engagement would not be enough to protect her. He had only one son, and two men could not protect the whole family. So they packed up their belongings and moved far away. Wagma was left alone with her new family. Her old house was empty. The fields were owned by her new family. Wagma's family was destroyed."

Zarina wept.

"If she'd had an older brother, this never would have happened," she continued. "A male sibling brings respect. Wagma did not want to marry. She had dreamed about being educated and becoming a doctor. Now she has no say in her situation. The Mirbaz family tells her what to do and when to do it. She must comply to avoid bringing shame to her husband. They demand complete control over her and they beat her to ensure it. That is all because of an old family dispute from long ago. Now in our little village, there is a new saying. If there is a serious argument between people, one might say to the other, 'I hope your family becomes like Wagma's family.'

"When my father saw what was happening, he decided to get a second wife so that he would have sons to protect our family from all that happened to Wagma's family. But he did not have enough wealth for an arranged marriage. A good wife, a beautiful girl, requires *walwar*, a high payment. So he decided to trade me for his future wife. He started to look for the second wife in many different families. He had issues and disagreements with many of them, that is, until somebody suggested to my father your uncle's family. The matchmaker told him about your Uncle Zahir's family.

"My father and your Uncle Zahir, my husband, are the same age. I am about fourteen years old, and one of his daughters is fourteen too. My father sent my aunts from our house to look at Zahir's daughter. They liked her. They did not communicate with her, but they saw that she was a healthy girl and that she did not have a disability. After all, it was her reproductive services that were important. This was not a love marriage.

"Some days later, your uncle's family came to my house to inspect me. On that morning, three women and one man came. I had just returned from the gudar (spring) with water, which, by the way, was no longer fun to do without Wagma. I was outside playing with my cousins when they showed up. I did not know who they were. The women called me to come closer. They asked me, 'Are you Raaz's daughter?'

"Yes, I am his daughter. Would you like to talk to my father? Let us go inside the house.

"They asked me, 'What is your name? Are you the oldest daughter? Come a little closer to us.'

"Yes, I am his oldest daughter, Zarina.

'Wow! You are Zarina? We are here to see you, not your father.' I smiled, but I was confused. I did not understand at all. I did not say anything. I just stood in front of them. They drew near to examine me. They stared at my nose, my ears, my eyes and my legs. They encouraged me, 'Can you walk a little for us? Walk to the edge of the field and come back.'

I thought they must be joking with me, but they looked serious as they stared at me. One said to another, 'Good. She is pretty.'

"I did not understand why they were discussing. They kept staring at me until they turned around to go into the house. I ran to the door and opened it for them. My mother was at home, but she did not come out to the guests. I saw my mother and ran to her. She was busy with the animals and cows. I said, 'Mom, there are some people here. They came to our house.' She burst into tears, which she wiped away with her scarf. I asked her, 'Is everything okay, Mama? Why are you crying?'

'Yes, I am fine.' she said. 'I have a headache.' My mother was quiet and sad, and I kept asking her who the people were and why they had come here. 'They are just visitors, and they will go back soon. We should prepare lunch for them. Prepare the tea.'

"I went to the kitchen to prepare tea, but the visitors kept calling me, 'Zarina, come here, girl.' I felt happy that they were so friendly and liked me for being pleasant with them. I kept returning to them again and again serving them tea, bread and food. I was trying to be nice with our guests, so I was chatting and smiling.

"Later, they asked me, 'Do you know everything about running a household? Do you know how to cook, how to take care of the animals, how to bake bread?'

"I answered, 'My mother does all the chores. I just fetch water. I do not know how to cook. I know how to play with the other children. I am thirteen years old.' I started to tell them about my games with other girls, my studies, and what I learned in the mosque, but they were not interested. They were interested in housekeeping responsibilities.

'Learn how to bake delicious bread!' said one of them.

'And learn how to be a good cook and take care of animals.'

"I said that sometimes I helped my mother, but I was mostly busy with games outside and with my studies. I left the room to join my mother in the kitchen.

"I was puzzled. Why did these guests care about my housekeeping abilities? I looked into my mother's eyes. She was very sad. I noticed she was not her usual friendly self with these people. For a moment it crossed my mind that those people were thinking about a marriage. But how could that be? My father loved me and he wouldn't do that to me, would he? Mother returned to the guests and everyone ate lunch, drank tea, and talked.

"When they left, I asked my mother again, 'Who are they? Why were they so nosy? They didn't care that I am a student. They told me to learn how to cook and take care of animals.' My mother said, 'Yes, it is time you learn. Most village girls already know how to do all their chores. You might marry one day.'

"I said, 'Mom, I am too young. I still have a lot of time. I will learn.'

"She said, 'The guests came to see you. They are considering you for a marriage.'

'What?' I started crying and ran to my room. I was so disappointed in my father's plan. My mother was also upset. I suddenly remembered that she had sometimes argued with my father. She had been telling him, 'She is still a child.' I had heard their arguments, but I had not understood what they were about. Now I understood. My mother was not worried about her husband taking a second wife, she was worried about me having to marry your fifty-five-year-old uncle to give him sons.

"I cried a lot from then on, but nobody listened to me. I really did not know the meaning of marriage to someone. And no one could help me. I was not able to tell my dad that I did not want to marry. I was a girl, and a daughter could never question or disobey her father. It was unheard of. I did not have that freedom. Whatever my papa decided was the rule. The only thing I was able to do was cry.

"I began to go to Ziarat's gravesite. Many people go there to pray for help. I saw sick people, people who couldn't walk or see. I went there many times, stood in front of it and prayed, first for Wagma and then for myself. I prayed not to be married. During those weeks, I visited a number of different graves with the hope that one of them would save me. I often left eggs for the malang (caretaker).

"At the same time, my family was busy preparing me for the engagement and wedding. Many times my mother and I cried together. I love my mother, and I knew that she disagreed with my early marriage arrangement. I did not want to hurt my mother's feelings, and I did not want to see her tears. I tried to be strong for her. I pretended that I was happy. I told her, 'Mama, everything will be good. It is noble to sacrifice myself for my family, so I have step-brothers that can protect us and can help my father with all his work.' But I was pretending, of course. Nobody wishes for a bad fate.

"Finally, the family gathered together for the engagement party. Your uncle's family invited us to go to their home. The traditional way in the village is that all the relatives go to each other's homes, and they say, 'Your daughter belongs to my family, and my daughter belongs to yours.' Of course, I was the bride, so I did not take part in that. For me it only meant that my wedding day was planned and would come soon, destroying my hopes and wishes. The engagement was completed, but I still hoped and prayed for some sort of intervention. But the wedding date was planned for as soon as I was old enough and ready to get married."

As Zarina was telling me the story, she wiped her eyes and her nose. Her voice cracked through her sobs. After a moment, she said, "I am sorry, I can see I have made you sad. I will cook your eggs and potatoes. The tandoor is ready for the dough now, so let me tend to it first."

She opened the tandoor. It was hot enough to bake the bread. She nervously knelt down at the tandoor to get the round pieces of dough to stick inside. Honestly, I was so afraid for her. I could see how frightened she was. She awkwardly reached deep into the hot oven to stick each flattened dough to the hot wall of clay. When the bread was baked, she reached down again to remove it, but pieces of the bread fell apart and down to the fire.

"My mother has twenty years of experience baking with tandoor, but I have no experience. How do I know if it is done? How should it look?"

Almost all the loaves fell apart and were burned. Their form was hardly round. The tears were streaming down Zarina's cheeks. She wiped them away again and again.

Aunt Fatima and Leila were crying more than Zarina had. They felt so bad for her, and my aunt feared for her daughter. What would her future be?

Aunt Fatima said, "I hope my daughter will not have such troubles." She hugged Leila and kissed Leila's head. To me she said, "Zarina shared all her secrets with you, everything that was in her heart. I can feel that. Zarina really trusted you. Did she finish the bread?"

"Yes, she did. She was very worried about what her husband would say about it. She was afraid that the family would be angry at her. I tried to help her myself, but I knew even less about it than poor Zarina."

"What happened next?" My aunt wanted me to continue.

"We should eat together now," Zarina said. "Let us go inside." I grinned and nodded in agreement. Because of the watch dog, I was not able to go back to the room. I did not move. She took the bread inside without me and came back with potatoes, pots, oil, and all the other ingredients she needed. She picked up three eggs and said, "One for me. Two for you."

"No, two for you, and one for me," I countered.

"City boy! You should learn our village life. Men always have more than women. Men always get the best and the most. Men are kings, and we are their slaves. I wish I were a man.

"Whenever Wagma and I saw a rainbow, a legend from our village always came to our minds. The legend says that if a woman crosses the top of the rainbow, she becomes a man. You are lucky that you are a man. Please, do not stop school. Study hard! Become a doctor."

While she was cutting the potatoes, she said, "I will tell you more about what happened after my engagement. All those graves I visited did not help me get out of my predicament. For nine months I tried to learn how to cook, bake breads, and take care of the animals. It was not enough time. When there was just one week left, I said goodbye to all my friends. I packed my belongings and a letter from Wagma, brought to me by her cousin. In it, she wrote that she would miss me forever. She also wrote that her mother-in-law told her she would not be able to go out from her husband's house, and she would not be able to play with her friends.

"On the morning before the wedding, I was told that the women in my soon-to-be husband's family would come for shab-e-henna, the first of a two-day celebration in the village. Then this was my last free day. I decided for the last day of my freedom to play with my friends outside. I totally forgot about my wedding. I was delighted to be with them even though it was only for a short time. My friends tried to keep me happy, and they told me that they would miss me a lot. They said they might come to my new house and play with me there. I told them that they wouldn't be allowed. I gathered some of my toys with me to take to my new house.

"We played until late evening, when almost twenty people seemed to arrive from nowhere. They began to sing. They carried a tray of henna and candles. One of the women played the dira (drum). Everyone went inside the guest entrance. And there I was still playing outside in the back, dirty from head to toe. Until my mom and sisters called for me, I hugged my friends goodbye again and again. Finally, I walked to the door of the house.

"I really didn't know what I should do next. I was so hungry, and I wanted to eat something, but my mother said, 'There is no time to eat. Go take a shower and change your clothes.' My shower did not take very long. I came out, and waited in my mom's room for the women to join us. I began to cry as I had seen other brides do many times before. They came into my mother's room. I stood in the corner and felt very uncomfortable. They decorated my hands with the red henna. It was two in the morning. I never had my lunch or dinner. I was so hungry, but I couldn't leave my own party. Besides, they had covered my face with a big green scarf. There was no way to eat anything. The night was almost over. I walked to the kitchen at about four o'clock in the morning. I ate a little bread with yogurt.

"The next day, villager guests and relatives came to my house. In the afternoon, my fiancée and his relatives arrived. He came inside the room with some women, and it was the first time I had ever met him. He looked older than my father. His hair was all gray and he had a scruffy, gray beard. He bent over a little bit at his shoulders. I felt young enough to be his granddaughter. He was ready to take me to his house, so I pleaded with my mom to come with me to the new house. I was crying. My mom said, 'I cannot go there with you.'

At the same time, the same situation was happening with your cousin, who was being brought to my father's house. Each party of revelers crossed paths on foot. I was taken to a car, and my cousin was taken to one, too. When the cars came upon each other, both stopped and my father's new wife and I spoke through the windows. Her name is Zermina. We were the same age, but she was crying more than me. We crawled out of the cars to kiss and hug each other. At that moment, we both realized that we were just as miserable as the other. We were both being sacrificed to bring more males into each family. And it was a huge sacrifice."

Zarina paused, tears streaming down her face.

"It has been months since that day, and I miss my

family a lot. I am sure they miss me, too. Your cousin's family is worried about Zermina. She was just like me, a little girl with no idea how to be a wife or take care of a house, or all the other responsibilities that suddenly became hers. And she is always sick. She has asthma. She always coughs and has attacks. Her mother told me about this. Now, I pray for myself. I do not know what will happen next. I do not have the freedom see friends. I live very far from my old house."

The potatoes were ready to eat. She picked up the three fresh eggs. I felt so bad, I told her, "I am not going to eat anything." She said, 'Oh, sorry, I made you very sad. I should not have made you feel that way. Forgive me." She hugged me and said, "You may not be hungry, but I am hungry. Let's eat together." Out of respect, I nodded.

"I will not be able to eat two eggs," I said. "You should take two, and I will eat one."

She smiled and said, "Yes, I will do that." We had our lunch together. She asked me not to tell her family that the lunch was served so late. I promised. I ate my egg and potatoes with bread, then suddenly realized I had completely forgotten why I was there.

"I totally forgot," I blurted, "I was not supposed to be here so long. I have to hurry back. My uncle will be so mad. Please, give me the stone." I was beginning to feel as worried as she was, yet she tried to keep me there longer. She was happy to have someone to talk to. Somehow she knew she could trust me.

"Stay a little more. I will run to get the sharpener for you," she tried to persuade. She brought the heavy stone to me. She also had some sweets and dried fruit, which she put in my pocket and said, "When you take the sheep to the fields, you can eat these. Come back some times." She gave me a hug and led me to the doorway.

At the first hill when I stopped to rest, I set the heavy sharpening stone on the ground and looked back. Zarina was still standing there. I gripped the stone tightly and wrapped my arms around it. Then I crossed hill after hill until I reached my uncle's house.

It was becoming quite cold. My aunt and my cousin were still listening to me. Sometimes they cried, and sometimes they smiled. My grandmother came out of her room, saw the three of us sitting together and said, "This Kabuli boy is too talkative. Go to bed! You keep everybody awake!"

Fatima told her, "Yes, we are going soon. We are having tea."

She brought tea and an oil lamp. It was not very bright. We could hear the the wind pass through the tops of the trees. I was still not sleepy. I was hoping to hear about Uncle Shar Khan. I tried to make my story about Zarina shorter, but they kept asking me for more details, even though it seemed to make them sad. Finally, I asked my aunt why.

"I hope my daughter's life will never be like that," she said. "I hope that this baby I am carrying is a boy. If I have a son, then I can protect my girl by myself. Oh, but there is no hope because I have had four miscarriages already."

She had tried to find a doctor, but village men do not like to go with their pregnant wives to doctors because it is an embarrassment for them. Nobody cared about Fatima. I told her, "I am your nephew, and I promise that I will help you. I will take you to the best doctor. I will find the money to take care of everything."

She gave me a hug, and wrapped a blanket around my legs to keep me warm. "You are a silly, wonderful little boy," she said.

"You promised me that you would tell me about Uncle Shar Khan," I reminded her. "Please, what went on there two days ago?"

Chapter 4

"Okay, let me tell you something you may not know about Uncle Shar Khan," my aunt said. "You are very young, and you do not know much. Uncle Shar Khan is one of the bravest and strongest men in the whole village."

"Yes, I know that. He is the best."

"Okay, wait, I will tell you more," she said. "He has a lot of experience and talents that help him live in the village and deal with people. He is the only person that always wants to keep peace between people and families. Once a family starts a fight it escalates. It gets worse and worse from arguing to blows. Sometimes, it can lead to deaths. Enemies look for the strongest person in the family, the one who keeps all the family together. If they can kill that person, it will weaken his whole family. That's the best way for one family to take over the other. Uncle Shar Khan is one of those important people. He gets along with everyone. They admire and respect him. He is especially very kind to women and children. His family members, especially the younger generation, are not as peaceful and respectful as he is. Yet they all respect him because he is so good. They have a special place for him in their hearts because they love him.

"Unfortunately, many years ago, there were two

brothers, Pacha and Kareem. They were violent and brutal men. They had many brothers, nephews and uncles, which made them very powerful. They also had guns. Pacha and Kareem treated other people in our village very badly. They targeted weak families, those who did not have male members to defend them. Pacha and Kareem wanted to terrorize the village, so everyone would be too afraid to fight them. This went on for many years. Sometimes, Pacha and Kareem attacked people in their fields and beat them to steal their wheat, corn, and rice. There was no one who could stop them. The weakest families left the village for safer places.

"Eventually, Pacha and Kareem started threatening Shar Khan's family as well, but Uncle Shar Khan insisted on not fighting back. He kept his family members out of trouble with Pacha and Kareem. Shar Khan's family was not weak. They were strong enough to deal with enemies. But he insisted that they not fight the brothers. He wanted to find a peaceful solution.

"The situation between Shar Khan's family and Pacha's and Kareem's families grew worse and worse. Shar Khan's brothers Gwal and Hassan lost their patience and had a bad fight with Pacha and Kareem. After this happened, Uncle Shar Khan went to Pacha and Kareem to bring his apologies to them, but Pacha and Kareem were determined to find the brothers and kill them. They wanted revenge.

"One day, Gwal and Hassan went to weddings in a nearby village. Pacha and Kareem knew they were going, and set a trap. As Gwal and Hassan returned to their homes, Pacha and Kareem took shots at them. Gwal and Hassan managed to overtake them, get their guns and kill both Pacha and Kareem. That was very good news for everyone in the village except for Uncle Shar Khan's family. Uncle Shar Khan was furious and shocked by the murders by his own brothers. His plan to peacefully end the feud between families was destroyed. He was very disappointed and concerned about the negative consequences that would undoubtedly come to his family.

"Uncle Shar Khan still wanted to reach out to Pacha and Kareem's families to offer his apologies. Uncle Shar Khan was going to prove to their family relations that his brothers killed Kareem and Pacha in self-defense. However, Pacha's and Kareem's families refused to see him. They wanted revenge. That is the villager way. Even so, Uncle Shar Khan was willing to sacrifice himself in order to protect his family from the revenge that would eventually come if nothing were done.

"Pacha and Kareem's families left for Pakistan to prepare. Now, the situation became more dangerous for Uncle Shar Khan's family. He would have to carry his gun with him at all times to protect himself — Pacha and Kareem's relatives would be watching his every move.

"A decade or so passed and everything was calm until, one day, word was sent that Pacha and Kareem's family were ready to meet. They had become very poor and had lost quite a bit of their status. Uncle Shar Khan sent a messenger to find that family in Pakistan to tell them he wanted to oblige. They were interested.

"Representatives of Pacha and Kareem's families arrived to begin talks. This is how it was going to be done, for this is how it had been done for generations before them. There had never been a lawyer or a courtroom. Their feud would be settled as they had been for years and years. For many days, the feuding families invited the most important people from all around the village and from the families. They had solved many similar problems for many families for at least 40 years. All villages have one such person to do these settlements. But for Uncle Shar Khan's situation, a lot of people from far away villages were asked to come. It would be an agreement that all must follow, and no one could break."

"Pacha and Kareem's brother Didar relayed their terms. They demanded three million rupees (approximately fifteen thousand U.S. dollars) and two of Uncle Shar Khan's three daughters. They were only eight and six years old. As is the custom among our people, they agreed to wait until the girls reached their fourteenth birthdays before they would have to join their future husbands, but the rupees would be due on the day of the agreement.

"Uncle Shar Khan offered to give them more money instead of his daughters, and he asked for more time. They agreed to the extension, however, they would not budge on the daughters. That was the village decision. So he asked the villagers and the people for a guarantee that his daughters would not be abused by that family. He was given that guarantee. And if something were to happen with them, the village would take care of it.

"Once the guarantee was in place, Uncle began to focus on raising three million Afghani rupees. He went door to door to each villager's house to ask for a loan. He promised to pay them back. Some helped him but he hadn't gotten nearly enough. He decided he needed to sell his fields, trees, and livestock. He sold almost everything he owned.

"Four months later, he had raised two-thirds of the blood money, but he had nothing left to sell. He asked the village leaders to return. Finally, they came to his hojra (guest house), and it was decided that two million Afghani rupees would be sufficient for now. Uncle Shar Khan could pay the remaining debt at a later time. The deal was made. The two million Afghani rupees were turned over to Didar. Then two sheep were slaughtered."

"Oh!" I exclaimed, "I remember seeing those sheep tied up near the circle of men."

"That evening a barbecue was held," Aunt Fatima continued, "and celebratory bullets were fired. It was supposed to be over, yet these kinds of problems seldom ever are. Uncle Shar Khan's family is very poor now, and that makes them vulnerable.

"Now," Aunt Fatima said, "we should go to sleep. The day after tomorrow is your cousin's wedding. We should be prepared to go there."

"Is Uncle Shar Khan going to be there?" I asked.

"Of course."

Chapter 5

I was relieved to finally know the story behind what I had witnessed at Uncle Shar Khan's house, and that I would see him soon. But now I had new worries. I asked my aunt, "Has something like this happened before?"

"Yes, many times. A good example is Sanga's family."

"Who is Sanga?"

"Sanga was my best friend," she began. "She lived in the village at the top of the hill. She was my classmate at the mosque and best friend. She was very smart. We always met outside of the mosque to play together after our classes ended. Sometimes we danced and sang.

"One day, her dad, Hassad, got into a serious argument with a man in the Khalil family over which of them owned a field. This was not the first time that these two families had fought over the field, and as time went on, there were more disagreements between them. Words were exchanged and both sides offended. Every year the fighting grew worse. Eventually, several of the young Khalil men attacked Sanga's brothers and cousins. The villagers came and stopped the fight, but not before her brothers and cousins had badly injured two from the other family, causing a deep cut with a shovel in one man's head and breaking another's tooth.

81

"Hassad knew that once family arguments turn into physical altercations, it's only a matter of time before weapons become involved. He tried to solve the dispute and negotiate with the Khalil family. However, the Khalils were sworn enemies and refused to negotiate peacefully.

"Hassad met with the mashran (elders) of other villages. They warned him that it would be a costly settlement because of the knocked-out tooth and head wound. Hassad pleaded that his family was good and that it was only in self-defense that the unfortunate injuries occurred. Still, the mashran said, violence meant that retribution was in order. Hassad agreed to respect their decision.

"Some time passed before the mashran from several villages gathered. They decided that for the cut head, Hassad had to give two sheep and one hundred fifty thousand Afghani rupees. And Sanga, my friend, was to be given to the man whose tooth was broken in two years, when she was fourteen. The Hassad family accepted.

"Sanga became more depressed as each day passed. I was very sad for her, too. I thought that it was good that she was still coming to the mosque to study, so I could see her. But now she did not want to play with any of her classmates. She was too worried about her future. Her dreams were gone. I tried to keep her happy, play with her, and take her to my house. I was able to change her mood for a little bit. Every time I returned from school, I talked to my mom about Sanga. My mother also felt sad about Sanga's situation, but she understood there was no way to change it.

"As the wedding date got closer, the Khalil family said, 'Sanga belongs to us. Enough school.' After that, Sanga did not go to the mosque to study anymore. I would still go to visit her at her house, though. She was worried about what was going to happen to her. 'My cousin broke my future husband's tooth! Maybe he will break all my teeth for this,' she said.

I reassured her that it could never happen, but could not give her advice because I did not have any experience. I told her to go to the shrines to pray for a good future.

"At the same time, I looked forward to the celebration that would come. I was happy that I would be able to go to Sanga's shab-e-henna. We would prepare Sanga's hair with honey and decorate it with shiny colorful foils. I wanted to put bangri (bracelets) on her hands, pacevan (a gold chain from nostril to earlobe) in her nose, earrings on her ears, beautiful shoes on her feet, a red scarf on her head, and beautiful rings on her fingers. It would be an entertaining party for the whole village. We would give all the guests food and gifts. The women would sing and dance together.

"One afternoon, while my mother was tending to her

chores, I asked her if I could have something new made to wear for Sanga's wedding party. I told her I wanted to buy some gifts for Sanga, too. My mother just gawked at me in disbelief, 'Are you crazy?' she asked. 'Sanga's wedding is not an arranged wedding! This is a revenge wedding. Sanga is only a payment for the broken tooth. There will be no party or celebration.' She shook her head and continued, 'Pray hard for your friend. It will be difficult for her.'

My aunt was crying as she told me the story.

"I took the clothes that I had chosen for myself and a clean notebook and went to Sanga's. Her hair was unkempt. Her clothes were disheveled. Her face was the same face I had always known, but somehow it had changed. Her skin was still smooth and her lips still pink, but there was no beautiful smile on them. All of her burden and fear showed. She said, 'I will miss you a lot. You are the only person who knows my feelings. Please do not forget about me when you pray. If I come to my father's house to visit, do you swear you will come? I will send my younger brother Nasim to let you know that I am there, so we can meet.'

"I promised her, but her words pierced through my heart. I pretended to be happy and encourage her. I told her not to worry about anything. She had brothers that could protect her. I asked her to be obedient and respect her future husband.

"She apologized for not being able to invite me to a wedding celebration. She said her husband's family would be coming to take her soon. She didn't know when, it could be day or night.

"I don't remember walking home. All I remember is crying and crying. I cried again a week later, on the day of her wedding. The skies overhead were dark and stormy. I was sure the bad weather had come because of Sanga's sadness. As the day fell to night, I worried about her more and more. The next day I asked my mom when I could see Sanga again.

"She answered, 'She just got married. The new bride should not go to her parents' house for several months. When the time is appropriate, I will go and ask her mother about her. I know she will be very sad.'

"My mom waited for two days to pass, and she went to see Tajo, Sanga's mother.

"When she arrived, Tajo invited my mother in for tea. My mother could see that Tajo had been crying a great deal for her daughter. They talked about how smart Sanga was, the fact that she had learned to read, and how she loved to help her classmates and friends learn. So many skills lost, they said.

"Her mother brought out books, notebooks and her writings to show my mother. She told my mother that Sanga really loved to study. Returning the books to their shelves, she

85

said, 'Now her books will sit on these shelves forever.' They took my mom to Sanga's old room. The walls were covered with her drawings. My mom said she was so surprised because her beautiful drawings looked like photos. It brought my mother to tears.

"Now all I could do was wait and worry about my dear Sanga until she could visit her family.

"Two weeks later, my mother visited Sanga's mother again. She was told that Sanga's father had seen her, and he said she is faring well. I was not convinced. I was sure new brides did not tell the truth about how they were treated in the beginning the marriage. It is very unusual that a village girl had a good life. I had heard things. I had seen things. I knew the customs. They liked to frighten the new wife and treat her badly to teach her to behave. This way she will be disciplined and never dare shame or disrespect anyone in her new family. But I had to wait until I saw Sanga again and could ask her for myself. We were best friends. We knew each other's thoughts, so she would never keep any secrets from me.

"A couple of months later, Sanga's family informed us that she was in her mom's house. I put on my clean scarf and ran all the way there. Out of breath, I knocked at the gate. Then I saw her in a corner of the big yard of their house. She saw me, too, and ran to me. I felt like I was dreaming. We hugged each other. With my arms wrapped around her, I noticed that she had lost a lot of weight. We kissed each other's cheeks, then walked arm in arm to her room.

"We were happy for a moment, talking about our past lives. We reminisced about the laughter and fun we had in school. Then she closed the door and the windows. As she sat down, I noticed how sickly she looked. Before I could tell her I had missed her and worried about her, she told me, 'I was counting my days to see you and tell you about my new life. You are the only one I can tell.'

"She started to weep. 'What I guessed before the wedding was right,' she said. 'My husband is thirty years old. From the first night I arrived, he started beating me. He said, "My tooth was broken. The cost of my tooth will be equal if all the members of your family have their teeth broken." I am so afraid of him. He calls me names and yells at me as he whacks me in the head. My mother-in-law does the same. Not one of them calls me by name. My husband calls me a cow and sometimes a donkey. I am all alone. No one treats me with any drop of kindness. The small children are scolded if they talk to me. As soon as I finish one chore, they give me another and another. I am worried about how much my husband will beat me tonight. He does not let me get any rest. He climbs on top of me when he wants me and then kicks me out of the room when he is done with me. I have no blanket or pillow in my room. There isn't even an old mattress for me.'

"I told her that she should tell her parents everything. She responded, 'No, I mustn't! If I tell, it is a dishonor to my husband and his new family. It will bring shame to my family for not being a good wife. The two families will start fighting with each other again. I love my brothers and my family. I do not want anyone to get hurt or worse. It is better to keep everything secret. Please, do not tell anything to anyone! I am carrying his child now.'

"We were in her house for the whole day," Aunt Fatima continued. "I had gifts for her, new clothes and a pair of shoes. She gave her books to me and she said, "Nobody will use these.' She gave me some drawings with her pens and pencils. Our time together flew by. As I said goodbye, she asked me again to not say anything to anyone, and I promised her.

"Mother and I left the house and came home. I asked my mom what could happen to Sanga when she gave birth. Mother cautioned me not to expect to see Sanga for a long time."

"After a month, my mom went to her mom's house again. Tajo said she had told Sanga's husband that he should take better care of her. He became angry. After that, Sanga was not allowed to visit her parents.

"Tajo said that they tried and tried to visit her, but there were always excuses. They tried sending her brother Naseem. When he got there, he was told Sanga was taking a shower. He waited for a long time, but never saw her.

"Seven months passed. Finally, my mother received word that Sanga had given birth to a baby girl. 'I wish she had had a son,' my mother said, 'At least a boy would have been a good gift for the family from her.'

"I knew that when a new bride gives birth to a baby girl, her life becomes worse. I feared that Sanga's life was in danger. So I decided then to tell my mother that Sanga's new family had been beating her. My mother was shocked.

'Why didn't you tell me before?' my mother demanded. 'Did you see any bruises to show that these beatings really happened?'

"I said, 'Yes, there were black and blue marks and bruises all over her body. Her in-law family warned her not to tell anyone or it would get worse, and she made me promise that I would not tell anyone.'

"She said, 'If we do not let her family know, we will not forgive ourselves, and we will be guilty forever. It is better to go to her mom and tell her about Sanga. Hopefully, they can help her.'

"A week later, my mom visited Sanga's mother again. Tajo hadn't seen Sanga for some time. Tajo had been infected with tuberculosis months earlier, and its symptoms made her unable to travel long distances. Her son refused to go. He did not like to deal with that family.

"My mother said, 'Please forgive me, Tajo. I know this is none of my business, but I care about Sanga as if she were my own, so I must divulge what I know.' Then, my mother shared some of what I'd told her.

"Tajo decided that she would go to Sanga immediately. She asked her husband to go with her because he was the most patient of all the men in their family. Naseem disapproved of her plan and insisted that he go with his mother, but Tajo refused. The parents would try to bring Sanga back to their home, at least, for a few days.

"When they returned, Tajo recounted the trip to my mother, who informed me.

"From the start, Sanga's mother knew something was going on. The family said Sanga had gone to see a doctor because her baby was sick. Sanga's mother said she would wait. Tajo was a smart lady. She tried to be cordial.

"There were children in the house, and when nobody was around, Tajo asked one of the small ones about Sanga's location. The child said that Sanga was in her room. Tajo

90

confronted Sanga's mother-in-law, and she agreed to take Tajo to see her daughter.

"Sanga was sitting in the corner holding her new infant. She kept her face covered. Tajo ran to her and took the baby from Sanga because the baby was crying. She asked Sanga why she was covering her face. Sanga did not answer. Tajo forced her to remove her scarf. When she lifted her scarf from her face, Tajo saw that Sanga's lips were black and blue. Her two front teeth were missing from her mouth. Tajo kept calm and gently kissed her daughter's cheeks. She asked what had happened. Sanga's mother-in-law said that Sanga had fallen off the roof when she was gathering dried vegetables. Sanga nodded in agreement. Tajo kept her doubts to herself not wanting agitate the mother-in-law.

"Tajo asked them if it would be all right if they could take Sanga to her father's house for a couple of nights. Her mother-in-law said they should discuss the idea with Sanga's husband and her father-in-law.

"The whole family disappeared from the women's part of the house to make their decision. Only small children stayed behind with Sanga. Tajo offered chocolates that she carried in her pocket to whomever could tell her what had happened to Sanga. Eager for the chocolates, several children said that they saw that her husband beat her. They saw Sanga cry.

"Sanga's mother-in-law returned to say that Sanga would be permitted to visit her father's house for a night or two. Tajo agreed. Sanga's father, Hassad, who had been waiting in the guest room all this time, still had no idea what was happening.

"Sanga scooped her baby in her arms and walked toward the guest room, not bothering to change from the ragged, dirty clothes that she had on. She asked her mother not to say anything to Hassad. Tajo agreed.

"As he hugged and kissed her, Hassad told Sanga he was disappointed she had not come out to see him sooner. Sanga did not respond, but her father kept asking questions. She did not give any answers. Tajo responded for her.

"As they were walking toward their home, they stopped to rest under an apricot tree. Hassad told Sanga that there was no one around, she did not need to keep hiding her face from him. Tajo said that Sanga was embarrassed because she had injured herself clumsily falling from the roof. Hassad opened her chador, saw the bruises and missing teeth, and insisted that she tell him the truth.

'I fell from the roof, Father,' she lied.

'Sanga, only your face is hurt from such a fall?' Hassad asked. 'It's not possible. You mustn't hide the truth, or it will happen again and again. How can I protect you if you don't tell me?'

"With tears in her eyes, she said that her husband, brother-in-law and father-in-law had been beating her. She revealed all the terrible details of her life. She described the time she fell asleep while cooking and burned the pot, and how her husband beat her with a stick, knocking out her teeth and leaving a bleeding gash on the back of her head.

"Her father flew into a rage. He swore he would go back and show her husband how it felt to be beaten so badly. But Sanga begged her father not to go. Tajo also pleaded with him, telling him they had to take care of Sanga first. He finally agreed and they headed for home.

"When they arrived, all Sanga's aunts and cousins gathered to welcome her. Sanga hid her face as much as she could. They asked questions about the bruises but she made excuses. Sanga's parents were worried about the reaction of the young men in their family. They would want to fight Sanga's husband just as Hassad had wanted to do.

"That evening Hassad asked Sanga's brother, uncles and cousins to sit down with him. He told them the truth. Of course, they wanted revenge, but Hassad insisted that too much blood had been spilled already, and, this time, things would change. He shared his plan. Sanga would stay at home. They would take their plight to elders of the village, who would meet again to decide how to handle it.

"When Khalil came two days later to take his daughter-in-law back, Hassad explained the situation. He said that Sanga would stay with parents until the elders made a decision, and sent him away. Khalil left in a rage.

"One afternoon, Naseem was working in the fields by himself. This was a dangerous time to be alone, but Naseem was naïve. Sanga's husband and his two other brothers brutally attacked Naseem and left him bleeding from a wound in his head. Naseem stumbled back to the house. His cousins rushed him to the hospital, but Naseem had lost too much blood and died.

"After this happened, in order to avoid more violence, Sanga's family left the village and moved hundreds of miles away to Pakistan. They might stay there forever. That was the result of the agreement between these two families. Now, let us wait to see what will happen to Uncle Shar Khan."

"Now," Aunt Fatima said, "you must go to sleep! Give me your clothes to wash. There will be a big wedding party in your house. Your cousin is getting married. You will see your Uncle Shar Khan."

Chapter 6

The next day, I was counting the hours, excited about the wedding. I overheard several conversations about my cousin's wife, Latifa. They said that she had some kind of mental problem. She always wanted to be alone. My aunt said, "When I met her, I realized there was something wrong with her. She sat and played with a newborn lamb the whole time I was there. I wondered how she would live with my cousin and if she would be able to deal with his parents. They were very cruel people. She was always screaming in her house. She always beats her sons' wives when they made mistakes. Her husband was even worse. God bless her! I will keep her in my prayers."

On the day of the wedding, I put on my freshly laundered clothes. My aunt used a bit of shalsham oil to make my hair look shiny. Against my protests, she pinned a hand-sewn flower made from white cloth to my shoulder. "We'll make you look like a villager," she laughed. Leila and her sisters were dressed up for the wedding, too, complete with shiny kamises down to their knees, covering their loose pants, and with red and green scarves covering their heads.

Off we went through the fields on our way to our cousin's house. I began to play with Leila and her sister until

Aunt Fatima admonished me, "You mustn't play in the middle of the village. You are the man of this group. You must walk ahead." I felt very special, very grown up, like a *marakchi*, decision maker!

When we reached the shaky wooden bridge, I lost my bravery, but my aunt reminded me I was Uncle Shar Khan's nephew and I mustn't bring him shame. I hid my fear and crossed over it as quickly as I could. I looked straight ahead, not daring to look down at the water.

In the distance, we could see that a huge crowd had gathered in front of the house. Several men were tending huge black pots over wooden fires outside the gates. The sounds of the music and singing were everywhere. The beat of daira played background to girls singing.

Young boys whom I remembered from school were the first we came upon. They called, "Hey, Kabuli Boy! What are you doing here?"

"I will punch you guys in your face!" I shouted. "This is my aunt's house. If you do something to me, I will not give you food."

A couple of hours later, I saw Uncle Shar Khan coming. He looked so stylish. He was wearing a brown vest over a white kamiss with matching pants. On his head, he wore a white cap. Around it was wrapped a black silk lungee that was twisted around his cap several times and came down over his left shoulder, hanging to his knee. He was walking several meters ahead of the women of his family, just as my aunt had instructed me to do. I called to him.

He replied, "Come here, my big, strong nephew! Where have you been?"

"You are asking me where I have been?" I responded. "You used to come to our house every day. Now you never do. Why not?"

"Do not be upset," he said as he picked me up. "I have been so busy."

"Guess what I have done! I led my whole family here myself!" I said proudly.

"Wow! You have become a big man!"

I looked at his shoulder. There was no pistol. No Kalashnikov.

"Where is my gun?" I asked. He held me in his hug, and carried me as he walked. "No more guns and pistols," he said. "Now, I will carry you on my shoulders."

"But you promised me that you would give me your pistol."

"I promised you, and I will give it to you."

We walked through the house. A lot of people were there. Most of them were elders, the marakchians and older family members. Uncle Shar Khan greeted and hugged every single person. I walked with him, so everybody gave me their hands, too. Uncle Shar Khan was given the special place of honor. I sat with him in the front of the room across from the door where children usually sat and played. I stuck close to his side among the elders. I asked him so many questions, and he answered every one of them. Tea was brought on a tray with chocolates. He picked up all of chocolate and put it in my pocket. We each had a big cup of tea. He was talking with other people, but he was also talking to me. After our tea, large quantities of rice, beef and loaves of bread were carried in and served. He made sure I had more than a sufficient amount of beef on the plate we shared.

Then we were ready to pick up the bride and bring her back to her new husband, my cousin. There were at least three hundred villagers taking part in the procession. I walked with Uncle Shar Khan. The groom walked with us. There was a lot of music and dancing along the way. We smiled and laughed.

When we got to the bride's house, they gave us a cloth napkin full of dried fruits and chocolates. A beautifully decorated egg was given to each guest. We stayed there for a couple of hours. I stayed close to Uncle Shar Khan, not saying a word so that no one would hear my strange accent.

Finally, the women were ready to walk back to my

cousin's house. They had been preparing the bride and themselves for the celebration since the night before. The bride came out through the big wooden doors. She cried so much at the door of her mother's house, you could here her sobbing over the guests' voices. To be honest, I cried a little bit, too. I felt so bad for her. The procession to my aunt's house began. When we came back to my aunt's house, guests slowly started leaving. Meters of colored cloth wrapped in plastic were given to each guest. Children got sweets and decorated eggs.

As evening fell, I said goodbye to Uncle Shar Khan. I watched him lead his family back until they disappeared over a hill. As was the custom, very close relatives stayed overnight one or two days to help the families clean up after the party. Our family spent the night at my aunt's house, too.

The bride was sent to the women's quarters, where a special pedestal was arranged for her. It was made from stacks of rugs. She was wearing a green chador that covered her from head to toe. A bridesmaid sat by her side to assist her. Each time another guest entered, the bride would stand. Again and again. How tired she must be, I thought to myself. Woman after woman would lift the green cloth to see her face. As was the rule, she had to keep her eyes closed, never knowing who was peering at her.

I also wanted to see the bride. I wanted to see for myself

if she was truly strange. I walked around her but did not get very close because I was a little afraid. I remembered my aunt's words and was scared that she had a mental problem of some sort. When I got close, her face was completely covered, she opened her chador ever so slightly. I saw only one of her eyes look down at me. She whispered to me very softly, "Boy! Come here." I timidly got closer to her. She did not look crazy to me. She had a little smile. She asked me if I liked chocolates. I said, "Yes I do." She put her hand in her pocket, pulled out some chocolates, and she gave them to me. I did not get the impression that she was deranged or unbalanced.

The next day we said our goodbyes to everybody. The poor bride was still sitting where I had seen her the night before. I went up to her to say goodbye. She replied, "I will have some more chocolates for you next time. You must come back." I promised her that I would be back soon. I left the house with my aunt and cousins.

"Aunt, you told me that my cousin's wife is crazy," I said. "She is not. She gave me chocolates. She is very kind! I promised her that I will meet her again soon."

She blasted back, "I know all about what you did and said! You sat with Uncle Shar Khan and the elders there. You asked the bride for chocolates. What did you do? You embarrassed me!" I was surprised to hear the anger in her voice. I explained that I did not ask for any chocolate, but my aunt was not listening to me at all. She added, "I did not say she was crazy. I told you she has a problem."

Each time we crossed over a field, my aunt stopped to rest. She was six months pregnant by then and was ill. She was suffering from a kidney ailment, which no one understood at that time. After our long walk, we arrived home.

After the wedding, life returned to normal. I still had to take my sheep to the pasture. Every day turned into the next. Sometimes I ran to Uncle Shar Khan, but he was very busy now. He visited once or twice, but he was occupied trying to pay off the remaining million rupees he owed. He was adamant he would pay this off.

Every day I asked my aunt, "When can we go to visit Latifa?" She told me, "This coming week." Two or three weeks went by. During this time, I began to feel sick. I got little headaches and felt as if I would vomit. I complained of my symptoms to my aunt and grandmother. They dismissed it as having over-celebrated at the wedding. I continued to do my work and ask about our trip to Latifa's.

One day, Aunt Fatima announced, "We will go to Latifa's house the day after tomorrow." I was so happy because I had finished all the chocolates from the wedding party. I thought I might get more chocolates.

When the day to visit my cousin's wife came, I had a fever and chills, but I didn't tell anyone how I felt. On the way to my aunt's house, I didn't look well. My aunt put her hand to my forehead, "You're burning up. You have a fever. You probably ate something bad. I will take you to the Khojali's shrine. It is only a little way further. It will make you healthy again."

We went to the tomb. There were pieces of rock salt and ashes on trays on his shrine. My aunt gave me a piece of the salt and some of the ashes to eat. I did as I was told and we went on our way.

Upon our arrival to my aunt's, I still had a headache and fever. My cousin said that some other families had the same symptoms. "Take him to the Hazrat Shrine," my cousin said. "It has more power to cure him." But when the women started talking, I sneaked away.

I looked throughout the house for Latifa, but she was nowhere to be found. Next, I searched outside. I saw a woman far away in a field and began to watch her. She was tending the animals. Sometimes she sat. Sometimes she stood. It continued for a long time. I wanted to join her, but there was a small river between my aunt's house and the field. The only bridge was made from two long tree trunks lashed together with cable. Clay mixed with dried grass kept cut limbs set perpendicular over the logs. There were no sides to it, and no hand rail.

I mustered up all the courage I had, and told myself that no matter what, I had to cross it. And so I did. I continued on through a field. In front of me there were a lot of cows and donkeys. They were much bigger than me. I was frightened as I passed through to reach her. Her face was totally covered, but when she saw me she smiled and waved for me to come to her, and I knew it was Latifa. Up close, she looked very tired and worn out. Her face was all red, and she appeared to be sick.

She questioned me, "You look so weak. What is wrong?"

"I do not know," I said. "My aunt told me I have a little fever but I will be okay. My aunt took me to Khojali Shrine. What about you? Haven't you gone to a shrine?"

"I am a new bride," she said. "New brides do not go to shrines or to doctors. It would create gossip among the villagers and bring disrespect to my new family. The neighbors would talk behind my back and say I am sickly. That would reflect badly on my new family."

"You should go inside to get some rest," I said.

"No, I must work hard and finish with the animals. Most of my day is here. Your aunt will not let me go inside."

"But you can barely walk. You must have more fever than me." I remembered the salt and ashes in my pocket. I took them out, and I put them in her hand. "These are from the shrine," I explained. "On my way back, I will stop at the same location, and I will get more for you as well. Please eat them."

She put them in her mouth. "Thank you," she said. "I am sorry. Today I have only one chocolate for you. I promise if I locate more, they will be yours next time you visit. If you go to another shrine, take more salt and ashes for me, too."

We spent the afternoon in the pasture with the livestock. Then she milked the cows in the barn and used a shovel to clean the stalls. I helped. After that, she formed cow paddies and stuck them on the wall to dry to be used like firewood.

"Atal, lunch is ready. Come!" someone called from the house. I invited Latifa to come with me. She declined. "No, I have a lot of work to do. Go and eat!"

At the bridge, I looked down at the water. It was moving so fast, and my head was spinning from the fever and headache. I hailed my cousin to help. "Kazem! Come here and help me cross the bridge." She ran up to the opposite side of the bridge from where I was and began to tease. "Look at you! Frightened like a baby! You are a big man? Huh! I can cross this bridge with my eyes closed."

"Please, you see I have a fever and headache."

"They said you ate too much chocolate. That is why you are sick. Go jump in the water. You will feel better."

104

I decided to cross the bridge by myself. She met me in the middle of the bridge and held my hand. She pushed me toward the edge a little to frighten me, and then she pulled me back to center.

"I've got you! Don't worry," she teased, and then began to push and pull again and again. I screamed, but finally, we crossed the bridge and walked to the house.

Lunch was ready in the *dallan*, summer kitchen. A cloth for the meal was laid not far from the tandoor. There were eggs and slices of buttered bread in fresh milk. There were also warm potatoes, yogurt and corn bread. My aunts and my cousin warned, "You should not eat any eggs or anything with oil." They gave me corn bread with yogurt instead. I took a bite of the corn bread and began to chew it, but I was not able to swallow it. I lost my appetite because I saw Latifa's face in the bowl. She had told me she hadn't eaten anything since the day before. I did not eat at all. I just wanted to sleep.

After lunch, we thanked our hosts and prepared to go home. Aunt Fatima asked me if I had seen Latifa. I nodded and pointed toward the pasture where the barn was. Together we crossed the bridge. We found Latifa sitting there, holding her head. My aunt kissed her cheeks, then laid the back of her hand against Latifa's forehead.

"You are very, very sick," my aunt said. "I wish I could

get you some salt and ashes from the shrine."

"This sweet little boy already gave some to me," Latifa replied.

"Oh, that is good. Keep eating the salt and ashes. They are miraculously powerful. I am sure you will get better. I will try to come back to check on you. Hopefully, you will get better soon." With that, my aunt said we should go because it was getting late. We stopped at the shrine for more salt and ashes, at the bottom of every hill to rest. We were both so sick.

Back home, my regimen of salt and ashes continued, but my fever, headache and vomiting got worse. Some of the village women came to my uncle's house, and they told my aunt, "That little fellow is very sick. You have got to take him to the Hezrat Shrine. Most people who were very, very sick survived after the pilgrimage to Hezrat."

Five days later I was worse, so my cousins accompanied me to Hezrat. I could barely walk. We climbed up the sacred site. They put me on top the monument, where I collapsed. My cousins thought I would be fine. I was not. I was dying. Twenty minutes later, I woke up in the middle of a bad dream about the gravesite. It was so quiet and dark, and I was delirious with fever. I was not able to scream because I did not have any energy left. I tried to reach my cousins. They came to me and held me up. One of them took some salt and put it in my mouth and said, "We think you are getting better now. Now you will be healthy. Let's go home and put you to bed. You need to sleep." It took us two hours to get home.

My uncle's family hoped that the power of the shrine would soon help me. But the sickness grew worse and worse. My uncle Dawood was very busy. With me unable to take the sheep to pasture, he worried about them getting enough to eat. He came to me where I had been lying for days and said, "I think you are better now, but you are weak because the whole day you sleep. If you walk a little outside, you will regain your strength. The fruit is ripe and ready to be picked. Take some apricots from the trees. You'll be like new."

I do not remember all his words, but I recall that I was not able to open my eyes. He brought a cup of cold water and poured it over my head. It startled me awake. I felt petrified. Smiling, he took me by my hand and pulled me away from my bed. Then he let the sheep out, and said, "I am sure you can take care of the sheep. Walk! walk!"

In a daze, I walked and bent down to the ground under a tree. It was such a hot day. The wasn't a cloud in the sky to shield me form the hot son. I sat under the tree in one of the fields. I thought I heard the sound of Uncle Shar Khan's voice calling to me. "Hey nephew! Don't you want to visit with me?" Was I dreaming? Since the first day my sickness, I'd had a recurring dream that he would come to me. His voice got closer. "What is this? You aren't coming to me for a hug? I have tea and bread for us. Sit up. What is going on with you? Are you sick?"

He hugged me, and took me to my uncle's house. "He needs to be taken to the doctor immediately," he declared.

"We took him to the greatest shrines," my aunt said. "He will recover soon."

"He is dying," Uncle Shar Khan protested. "And you are still waiting for the shrine to cure him? I am taking him to the local doctor to have him examined. If your husband Dawood comes, tell him that we are at the doctor."

I still thought I was dreaming. He told me, "Rest your head on my shoulder. I am sorry that I didn't come to your house last week. I asked your aunts and uncle where my big man was. They told me that you had a little headache. I had no idea you were this sick. I am so sorry." He kissed my cheek and he squeezed me in his arms.

The doctor was four villages away. It took Uncle Shar Khan an hour to carry me there. The doctor examined me and said I had to be taken to the clinic in Paktia right away. He suspected that it was a case of malaria, but did not want to prescribe any medication that could prevent me from being treated later.

Paktia was a four-hour drive from our village. All afternoon Uncle Shar Khan stood by the dusty dirt road, waiting for a car or tractor to come by. After almost three hours, a friend of Uncle Shar Khan's stopped his truck for us. My uncle lifted me inside and climbed in after. We passed through the forest on a mountain road for hours.

We got to the hospital around sunset. There were patients everywhere, even sleeping on the floor. Only two doctors were on duty. The doctors slowly took patient after patient. It took hours before it was my turn. The doctor came into the examining room, checked me, and said, "He needs urgent care." He ordered blood tests, and a technician came to draw blood. We waited for the results, which showed that I was highly infected by this time. He told me, "You are lucky you are still alive, poor little boy."

To Uncle Shar Khan, he said, "Children his age can be killed by malaria in just two weeks. He will have to be hospitalized. He needs injections and an IV. He is badly dehydrated and severely anemic."

My uncle stayed with me the whole night. I would wake up and try to talk, then fall asleep mid-sentence or before I could hear his reply. In the morning, I was given another IV and told I would remain in the hospital for one more night. I was starting to feel better. But the doctor told Uncle Shar Khan I need a medication called Chloroquine. It was expensive, the doctor said, and we'd have to travel to Khost to get it. Uncle Shar Khan assured him that we would, if the doctor provided a prescription.

The following day Uncle Dawood showed up to confront my uncle. "Why did you take Atal to the doctor? I don't believe in doctors."

"Look at him," Uncle Shar Khan responded. "He's so much better after one day of medical treatment."

"Sure, he is better now, but it is not because of these doctors. It is the power of the shrine healing him. Let us take the boy and go home. You are wasting your money and your time."

Uncle Shar Khan chuckled. He said, "Okay, you might be right. The important thing is that my nephew is getting better. His fever is going down and he can eat again." That was true, I was eating a lot, but my headache remained. The following afternoon, loaded with tablets and syrup, I was released and Uncle Shar Khan was given the prescription for Chloroquine.

"Give me a couple of weeks," he told me. "I will go and buy the medication. That will work."

We returned home. After a couple days, I resumed taking care of the sheep again. Uncle Shar Khan visited me every day. He always said, "Hey, my big nephew. I will get your medication for you very soon. Do not worry."

The medication I was taking at the time helped me. I supposed if I were able to save some syrup and tablets for Latifa, they would certainly help her, too. It had been almost three weeks since I had seen her. How happy I could make her with this small gift.

In the meantime, my Aunt Fatima's health was deteriorating. She was pregnant and she had some sort of problem with her kidneys although I didn't know that at the time. I asked her, "Can we go to Latifa's house? You remember she was very sick. I want to share my medication."

"Are you crazy, boy? Uncle Shar Khan said that the doctor advised that you must finish the whole course of medication. If you skip something, you will relapse and get sick again in no time!"

"I have been taking all my medication for three weeks. I am okay. At least I can save a little bit."

My aunt admitted that she was worried about Latifa too. "We haven't heard anything from there," she said. "I am sure she was sick before she got married. I heard that there was malaria in her village. Several people died from it! I hope she is okay. I will send my daughters. You can go with them. Take her some eggs. She can eat them, and you can enjoy yourself at your Aunt Suheila's house. Do not stay overnight night, though. Your uncle will be so mad at you if you do not return and take the sheep out."

On the way, my cousins asked me if I wanted to return to the shrine for "treatment." I smiled and said, "You, people, are crazy. There are just dead bodies there."

When we arrived, I found Latifa in the corner of the animal pen. She was in a terrible state. Her clothes were filthy, and she smelled awful. I was stunned that she didn't hide her face from me as she had always done. One of her eyes was swollen as if she had been hit. Her skin was yellow. She didn't seem to recognize me. She was murmuring something I couldn't understand.

I showed her the medication and said, "You have to take this. It will help you." Then I ran to find water for her. I saw a big pot used to transport the water from the river to the animal trough, took it, and ran down to the river. The water looked clean. I scooped some up into the pot, which made it to heavy for me to lift. My cousin Leila saw and came to help me lug it back to the pen.

I tried to put the medication in Latifa's hand but she

didn't know what I was doing and the tablets fell. So I tried to put the medication directly into her mouth, but Latifa was not able to open her mouth. I never thought this would be difficult. I felt frightened. Leila and I ran to my aunt's house for help.

"Oh, my cute nephew, come here," Aunt Suheila said as she kissed me. I did not know why they were so happy. "Latifa is in the barn," I said. "She is very sick. She cannot talk. I tried to give her some medication."

"Forget about her," my aunt said. "We heard that you were dying. You were in a big hospital."

"Yes, I am okay now. We must give our attention to Latifa. She is very sick. She is dying."

"We took her to the most powerful shrines. Be patient. It takes time for the power to work. The doctor did not help you, you know. You were at the shrines before the hospital, weren't you? We know they cured you. Everyone believes in the shrines' ability to save us."

"I got better with the doctor," I argued.

"Don't you dare say that. It's a sin."

"Okay, maybe the shrines did work, but why didn't I feel better? Why did I get sicker? At the hospital, I could feel the difference as soon as I was treated. The drips helped me a lot. The doctors also gave me a lot of injections. It is better to take her to the hospital."

"We will wait," my aunt said.

"But the doctor said that malaria can kill people in two weeks. Latifa has been sick for two months," I said trying to persuade them.

She smirked. "Okay, now you have become a doctor? Latifa will be fine."

I gave the medication to my aunt. "This is good medication. Give it to her," I pleaded. "I saved it for her." She looked at the packet. She said, "Oh, I love this medication. It helps me a lot. It can cure headaches. And look at this bottle! This syrup is good. I'm going to give it to my son. He is too skinny."

"No, it is for Latifa!" I protested. "I was supposed to finish all of the medication, but I saved it for her. Please!"

"You've become so skinny, too. We need some good food." She started preparing eggs for me. I said that I was not going to eat. I just wanted to go back home and tell my Aunt Fatima what had taken place. My aunt was kind. She would help Latifa.

I returned to the animal pen. Latifa was still in the same place and in the same position. She was able to open her eyes a little, but that was all. My cousins came along and looked at her face. "Somebody must have beaten her with a stick." Before we said goodbye, we promised that Aunt Fatima would come.

We went home. I expected my aunt to go to Latifa that day. My cousins pointed out that Aunt Fatima was sick, too, and that her baby was due soon. "Well, we will see. If she hears about Latifa, she will go," I said. "If she does not go, I will go to Uncle Shar Khan's house."

"Are you crazy?' Leila said. "He is a man. And he is not a close relative. He can't take care of her."

"What are you talking about?" I asked. "I am a man also."

She smacked me and said, "You are a small baby. You pretend that you are a big man."

"Latifa needs help. I know the tablets will help her if only Aunt Suheila will just give them to her."

"Latifa will never see them. Didn't you see how excited Aunt Suheila became when she saw the red packet? She said she would use them herself! And you had a lot of treatments, not just a few tablets."

"The doctor told me that this medication is very important."

"Really, boy! You may not have the same sickness she has. It might be something different. You think all treatments are the same?"

"I feel so guilty," I said. "I wish I took drips with me,

too."

When we reached the house it was almost evening. My aunt did not feel well. She was moaning. Still she asked, "How is Latifa?" I told my aunt, "Aunt, Latifa is very, very sick. She was not able to talk or open her mouth to take the medication I had for her. She was in the animal pen. I think she's been living with the animals in that pen for a long time. She was very dirty. There were some cuts on her face. Aunt, I felt so bad!"

"I will pray," Aunt Fatima said. "If I can get better, I will go to see her soon. But you see, I am not able to walk that far."

"You both need to see a doctor," I said.

"Who will take me to the doctor? I have already lost newborn baby boys because nobody takes me to a doctor."

"Aunt, I will take you. Please. I have some money Uncle Shar Khan gave me."

"Thank you! You are a big man. But we will just pray not to lose my baby."

The evening ended with uneasiness. Leila and I slept in the same room. The whole night we talked about Latifa and my Aunt Fatima. How can we save Latifa? We were just kids. Nobody would listen to us.

"Maybe Uncle Dawood can do something!" I said.

"If you were hoping that my father will help my mother,

116

you'd better get that idea out of your head. It's impossible. Mother told you she lost the other babies. That's because no one will help her. Even if he wanted to help, he wouldn't be able to, he is traveling this time of year." Traditionally, people buy sheep at the end of summer and keep them for the next year to replace those that will soon be ready for slaughter. Uncle was away with a couple of his male cousins to buy the sheep. I was the only man in that house. I had to take care of everything.

The next day Aunt Fatima seemed to be worse. I pleaded with her, "Please, let us go to the qabela (midwife). I will take you."

She said she was worried about leaving the house without Uncle Dawood's permission. Grandmother intervened. "Go to the qabela and take Leila with you," she said. "Go with Atal, he knows where the qabela is."

My aunt had difficulty walking. We had to walk slower and slower as we went. Finally, she stopped. Leila and I helped her sit down to rest in a field along the dirt road. We hoped someone would come by to help. After a long time, a tractor pulling a small wagon with women riding along came by. We waved him down.

"Who is your father?" he asked me. I knew he wouldn't know my father, so I told him I was Uncle Shar Khan's nephew. He knew my uncle, so he asked if we were okay. I said, "No, my uncle's wife is so sick. Could you please help us get to qabela's house?" He said, "Yes, I will help you."

The women got down from the wagon and helped my aunt up. They spread some blankets on the floor of wagon to make it a little more comfortable for her. The ride was very rough. We rocked back and forth for nearly an hour before he pulled up to our destination.

The women took my aunt inside of the qabela's house. I was told to stay outside. I walked around anxiously. It seemed to be taking forever. I calmed myself by remembering that I had gotten Aunt Fatima to someone who could help her. Now, she would be okay.

When Leila called for me, I rushed in with excitement. I couldn't wait for the good news I was expecting to hear. The qabela and Leila were waiting for me. The qabela took one look at me and exclaimed, "This is the man with you? This little boy? I need an adult, so I can explain your aunt's condition."

"You can tell me! I can take care of her."

"Is there anybody else with you? Somebody older? You should find someone from your family. Your aunt needs urgent care. Not only is she pregnant, but she is sick. She may need a C section to save her life and the life of her baby. She might need blood for a transfusion."

"Okay, I will find someone," I said. But the village was far, and it was dark now. I pulled Leila to the side. "Take this money in case," I whispered. "I don't want it to get lost. We may need it for the hospital." She was crying.

I told my aunt and the midwife, "I am going." She said that it was not possible to find the village, and tried to dissuade me from going. I told her I had to go. My aunt gave me her scarf.

I left the house and ran.

I knew that if I kept on the road, ran north, and found the river, I would eventually come to my village. I thought there was no point in going to Uncle Dawood's because he was out of town, so I headed to Uncle' Shar Khan's house.

Chapter 7

At first, I was very afraid. What had I gotten myself into? I turned my thoughts to why I was doing all of this. I thought about how important it was to me to save my aunt's baby. She was praying for a healthy baby boy because this would help her daughters. A baby boy would mean her husband wouldn't need to use her daughter in a trade for a second wife who could produce a son. Now I wasn't afraid. I felt brave.

As I ran down the road, I held my hands together, palms up, like I learned to do in prayer, and I asked God to help me and keep me safe. There was nothing on the road, no cars, no humans, no animals. I imagined in the darkness the shrines that I was so afraid of. I was terrified each time I passed by one. The nightmares I had when I was sick were fresh in my imagination again.

I finally reached the *dukanoona*, where all the village shops were located. I checked each shop for an open door. It was too late, all of them were closed for the night. I knocked on some doors hoping I might wake up one of the shopkeepers. Nobody came out. It was almost midnight.

I started walking to the village. No more shrines to fear, but there was still danger before me — my old enemy, the river. I was so afraid of the water, and the narrow little walkway across it. The thought of stepping out onto the shaky wooden foot-bridge scared me so much, it made me shake inside. I couldn't cross it. I backed away. I ran along the river bank to find a shallow part, where it would be safer to cross. I stepped in one foot after another. The water reached to my knees. The sound of the waves frightened me, but I kept going. Now the water reached higher. I felt it was going to pull me in, so I returned to the bank. Again and again, I tried to find the courage to cross. Once again I gingerly stepped into the river and began crossing. This time the water was up to my waist, but its current wasn't so strong. For my aunt, I thought! I made it to the other side.

The last danger between me and Uncle Shar Khan's house was the village dogs. I could not avoid them. I broke a huge stick and carried it with me to protect myself. My heart pounded in my chest, my mouth went dry. My plastic shoes were full of water, squeaking and squishing with every step.

Village dogs everywhere were barking at me. I ran and ran, so they could not catch me. I picked up stones, and filled my pockets for more protection. I had my stick in my left hand, and my right hand wrapped around one of the stones in my pocket. I was prepared. Only three fields further from his door, I was stopped. Dogs! They were coming too close to me, so I threw the stones one by one as I moved in closer to my destination. I tried to throw stones at my uncle's door to alert him, but none reached. The commotion woke up several villagers. They climbed to the top of a roof and shot a couple of warning bullets into the air. "Who's out there!" one called. More shots. I was afraid I was going to be shot dead.

Somehow I managed to call out, "Uncle Shar Khan!"

"What is your name?" the shooter demanded. I said, "Dawood's nephew, Atal!" He ran down and called back the dogs.

Through the dark, Uncle Shar Khan came running. His turban was not on. He picked me up into his strong arms, "What are you doing out so late? It's midnight? Have you gone crazy?" I was not able to answer. He took me inside. He saw my bleeding feet and wet clothes. By this time all the family was awakened by the fuss. One doctored my feet with oil and rags. Another burned something to make ashes and applied the ashes to my feet, too. Uncle Shar Khan's wife came with dry clothes. They brought me food with a glass of milk, and wrapped a blanket around me.

"Why did you leave your house?" they asked. "Did Uncle Dawood beat you?"

"I did not come from my home. This morning Leila and I accompanied my aunt to the qabela. She is sick. The qabela said to get help or Aunt Fatima or the baby will die."

"Where is she now?"

"She is still at the qabela's." The whole family looked shocked. With one voice, they asked, "You came here from there all by yourself?"

"Yes, I've been running all night."

"You are a big, brave man, my nephew," Uncle Shar Khan said. He turned to his family. "I told you people that he is a strong man. Look at him! Who can get here from over there?"

"We are really proud of you." they said.

I pushed away the food they offered. "There's not time to eat. She needs us urgently! Please help. Let's go back." I took the glass of milk and gulped it down.

Several male cousins dressed themselves for the trip, but I told them that we needed more people for blood donors. One of them got five more cousins in the compound to come along.

Uncle Shar Khan's brother brought the tractor with the wagon on the back to the big gate. Several men put blankets and guns in the wagon, and then everyone climbed in. They told me, "You do not have to go with us. You need to rest."

I said, "I must see my aunt. I promised her."

They said, "All right, then," and pulled me in.

The tractor bumped slowly along the dirt road. The back

123

of the wagon swayed as the tractor was steered around the ruts that could be avoided. My feet began to ache. Somehow I managed to curl up next to Uncle Shar Khan and fall asleep.

It was almost sunrise when I woke up. I saw Leila at the door of the qabela's house. She was so excited when she saw us. She ran in to announce our arrival then came back out.

"How is my aunt, Leila?" I asked. She was crying.

"She is not able to talk."

We found my aunt with the midwife, who spent the whole night at my aunt's side. She said, "I will go with her to the hospital. I can help."

My aunt was carried to the wagon. She lay on the blankets. The qabela, Leila and I surrounded her and covered her. It took four hours over rough dirt roads to reach the hospital. We drove through the big gates to enter.

In the hospital, there were a lot of patients. Aunt Fatima was taken into the examination room. We were told the surgeon would arrive in two hours, but it really took three. He looked like he had come directly from the fields. The qabela spoke to him. "You have a huge responsibility. Our patient needs urgent care."

"Yes, yes, yes," he said, as if shushing her.

"She needs more care than we give her here. You got her here too late. I suggest you take her to the hospital in Khost, which is eight hours away. That hospital has state-of-the-art equipment."

The doctor agreed. The family wanted to get word to Aunt Fatima's husband but the doctor said that if they waited much longer, neither the mother nor baby would survive.

Uncle Shar Khan said, "Okay, give me a little time to find a car." He went into the city, a little further from the hospital. After an hour, he returned in an old station wagon. The driver said we would not all fit. Uncle Shar Khan told his cousins to take the qabela back to her village. Uncle Shar Khan, Leila and I rode with my aunt.

By the time we had crossed the halfway point, she was very weak. She did not open her eyes or respond to our questions. Her condition seemed hopeless. Leila was crying again. She thought surely her mother was dying.

At midnight we reached the hospital in Khost. We were lucky. There were doctors on duty there. They examined her quickly and scheduled surgery. We were warned, "There is no guarantee either will survive because her condition is so advanced. You may have gotten here too late, but we will try our best."

They took her inside. Only Leila was permitted to be present. Uncle Shar Khan and I sat in the waiting room.

Through a loud-speaker system, the next patients were called, birth announcements were given, and calls for medications were made. We were so nervous. Uncle Shar Khan reassured me, "Everything will be okay. She will be fine. We will return home happy with a sweet new baby. Now you will have a cousin. You are a brave man. You helped your Aunt Fatima a great deal. You will go to heaven. Let us go to the pharmacist. They will bandage your foot wounds properly."

The pharmacist removed the broken plastic shoes from my feet. Jokingly, he peered at me through one of the holes in a shoe and asked, "Did you know you had such big holes in your shoes? What happened to your feet?" There were splinters of wood in both feet. His assistant removed them and he washed my feet with iodine. It stung so badly, but I held back my tears to show Uncle Shar Khan that I was a big boy.

Uncle Shar Khan shared the whole story with them. They looked at me with great surprise. The pharmacist congratulated me on my valiant effort and hugged me. Then they had some bread with honey and green tea brought in for us. As we sat down to eat, we were interrupted, "You are being called from the emergency room." We ran. The old woman who worked at the door met us at the entrance. She said, "They are calling you in."

Uncle Shar Khan told me to wait and not be afraid. The

doctor told him they needed blood. Then he rushed into to the waiting room and called to the people waiting, "Our patient needs blood. This is an emergency. We need your help." The room became silent. Then two men spoke up. "I can give blood, too," I said.

With a broad grin, Uncle Shar Khan said, "You are so tired. Look at your feet! You lost so much blood with your wounds. You have not eaten anything since the night before last. You are courageous, my big man, but there is no blood in your body to give."

He said, "I will go first. If my blood doesn't match, I will call you."

An hour later, the two men came back, but Uncle Shar Khan was not with them. They told me, "He is coming. His blood matches your mom's blood. Is she your mom?"

I said, "No, she is my aunt, but she takes care of me like a mom."

"This is a good hospital," one of the men told me. "She will be okay." They continued talking to me. My limited Pashto kept me from understanding them very well, but they were patient. They joked with me. They were in a very good mood because one of their women had given birth to a baby boy earlier that evening. They described the celebration they would make. Boosting my spirit, one man said, "You will have a cute male cousin. There will be a huge party, and people will come to your house to congratulate you and celebrate with you."

A nurse announced, "Congratulations, Jamal family. There is a daughter in your house." The family looked disappointed. No one congratulated them. A woman in the waiting room leaned over to them and said in a hushed voice, "It's okay. Be patient. God will give you a son next time."

Each time a son was announced, a huge crowd gathered round the father who grinned from ear to ear, showing his yellowed teeth. Everybody gave their congratulations. "Thank you, thank you," he would say. "May God give you nephews and sons and bring happiness in your houses. Thank God."

The nurses that made the announcement stood nearby to collect money given to them for giving the good news. The nurses divided the money amongst themselves. Door attendants stood in line for a small reward as well. Another girl was announced. Again no congratulations, no celebratory cheers, no money to reward any of the workers.

As I watched these rituals, I was so perplexed. I thought to myself that boys and girls are both humans. I had never experienced this before. It did not feel right to me. I surveyed the people around the room and outside anxiously awaiting their news. They were praying, "God, please, give me a son," or "God, please send good news." As the hours passed, I prayed, too, "God, please restore my aunt's health. Make her a survivor." I repeated it again and again. I held my hands before me, open in prayer. But I never asked God to give me a male cousin or a female cousin. Only their good health and survival were in my prayers.

When Uncle Shar Khan finally came out, he looked a little worried. He joined me on a bench. "Everything will be fine," he said. He thanked the men who had volunteered, and congratulated the happy families, "Congratulations! You have a baby boy in your house. You should be proud of yourself. This is good news."

Minutes later, the nurse on the loudspeaker called Uncle Shar Khan. "You stay here," he said. "I will be back. Maybe they need more blood." He ran. I could not sit another second, so I followed behind. The doctor met him at the door. "We are sorry," he said. "We could not save the patient. But God gave you a nephew."

When we returned to the waiting room, people asked Uncle Shar Khan, "What is the news?"

"I lost the patient."

"What about the baby?"

"The baby was saved."

"Is it a boy or a girl?"

"It is a boy," he said, and the congratulations began. "It will be fine. It is important to have a boy. You will marry again. Thank God you have a son. It is such a gift to you." I was looking at everyone thinking, "For these people, a newborn son is more important than his mother's death. A woman's life is fair sacrifice for a son."

In a subdued voice, Uncle Shar Khan said to me, "We will need a coffin for the body. I am going to go meet with a friend. You wait here."

When he came back, his friend was with him. They had a coffin that my uncle had bought with borrowed money. The cousins and Uncle Shar Khan planned our return home that evening, but we were stopped by the hospital.

"The baby is small. He must be monitored through the night. We will release him tomorrow," we were told.

At noon the next day, we asked for the newborn boy. We convinced the doctors that we had a doctor in our own village to care for the small baby. We had to take care of a dead body. We started driving back to our village in two cars, one for us and one for the coffin. Leila held the newborn all the way home. It took about ten hours. We got there at midnight. We knocked on the door of Uncle Dawood's home. Grandma was in a tizzy. She looked at me and yelled, "What have you done? I told you to be gone no more than a few hours, but it has been days!

Uncle Shar Khan stopped her. "It is midnight! You ought to be ashamed of yourself."

Then, Leila came through the doors. The car lights illuminated the area, and all eyes were on her as she carried the newborn child for grandma to see. "This is your brother," said Leila to her sisters, standing behind Grandma.

"Where is Fatima?" Grandma asked.

"Abu died in Khost."

Grandma and Leila's sisters began to cry. "Abu, Abu," they wept. Shar Khan went door to door to give neighbors the bad news.

Soon people from different villages came. They prayed for the dead body, and gave congratulations to my uncle for his new son. I thought about Latifa. I thought about my aunt. My poor Aunt Fatima was more concerned about Latifa's welfare than her own, even though her own death was near. I had to find someone to tell me about Latifa. I found one of my Aunt Suheila's children. "Cousin, how is Latifa?" I asked.

"Do not worry," she said, smiling. "You will be at her funeral very soon."

I asked Latifa's sister-in-law Murina the same question. She too told me it would not be long before I would be attending Latifa's funeral. She seemed to take pleasure in it.

Leila pulled me away. "My mom's last words to me were for us to go to Latifa," she said. "I am sure she needs to go to the good hospital, but two weeks ago, she was in very bad shape. I am not sure what will happen to her now. I have to figure out something to do with the new baby, so I can go to Latifa with you."

Although the hospital had provided us with dry milk for the baby, it gave him stomach aches, so a woman who had had a girl-child earlier was called in to be a wet nurse to the new baby boy.

My cousin arranged to leave the baby with her sister Gulapa and our grandmother so that we could leave the next morning. We ran through the fields to get to Latifa's house. We went straight to the animal pen. Murina and two other women were there, and more women from the village were also going there. We were just a few feet away when we saw Latifa lying on the ground. Her clothes were covered in dirt. The animals had peed all over her. The stench was intolerable. The women scolded us to stay away, but neither of us stopped. One of the women standing over Latifa ripped a piece of red scarf to tie Latifa's two index fingers together. Next, she pulled the piece of scarf around Latifa's head and tied it under her chin. It was then I realized that Latifa was dead.

(Years later, one of the women who washed Latifa's body would confess that she had suffered a terrible head wound — this is what the woman was covering with the red scarf. She had been struck in the head with a large stone. This apparently happened the same day that her father-in-law made an unusual visit to Uncle Dawood's. He stayed the whole night, which was unlike him.)

Leila and I decided to go back home. I ran, haunted by Latifa's face, the awful smell, and her filthy condition. The way she died was deplorable. We told our grandmother about what happened when we returned. By the evening, the dam came to announce Latifa's death. The next day the whole family planned to go to the funeral. I watched my grandmother. She did not look very sad. In fact, no one seemed to be grieving.

As was the tradition, her family had come to the husband's house to retrieve their dead daughter's body and return her to her father's home. Her family surrounded her. They had washed her body, and they put her in the coffin on a wooden cot tied together with rope. I was trying to get to her body to see it for myself. My cousin helped me to get there. She said, "Come. You were the only person that always cared about her. You shared your medicine with her. Come see her face for the last time." I edged my way to the front. I was afraid because her scary face in the animal pen was in my mind. It had haunted me all night. My cousin pushed me more. I stood at the top of her casket and I was amazed by her face, adorned with two yellow flowers. Her face was so beautiful. It was like the moon. She looked like she was sleeping. She seemed to be at peace.

We spent the night there. My head started to hurt again. I thought it was due to all the sadness and tension in this past three weeks.

We all came back with my youngest aunt, Zarka. She had come from a different village. She felt bad for me because I was so tired. I missed my Aunt Fatima a lot. I could not forget about her. Latifa's funeral affected me too. I felt homesick. I missed my parents and my big sister. I missed my home, and I longed to be back at school. I had fallen so far behind in my studies. I cried to Zarka that I wanted to be with my family.

Zarka stayed with us for a week to take care of the baby. At the end of the week, we pleaded with her to stay longer. Her husband came to pick her up though, so we asked him to let her to stay for one more week. I promised him that I would bring her back to his house, and he agreed, so she stayed for one more week.

During this time my Uncle Dawood was as sad as he was happy. It had always been his dream to have a son. My Aunt Fatima had the same dream. I still felt guilty. If I had taken her to the doctor earlier, she may have survived. I kept all the sadness within myself.

I often visited her grave. I stood there and apologized to her. I am sure she was happy because she had finally given birth to a baby boy. She had fretted over it for so long. I wished she was there to see her sweet son.

Little by little, there was happiness in my uncle's house. They were thankful for the baby boy. Especially when Uncle Shar Khan came to our house, it was an amazing time for our family. I remember the Tuesday Aunt Zarka was going to return to her home. Uncle Shar Khan stopped by. He made jokes and talked with everybody. He called, "Bring a huge pot of green tea, I am so tired. I came from the fields." My cousins brought tea. My aunt and he chatted. Zarka began teasing with Uncle Shar Khan, "You are very free man? You trust this Didar family? They are not honest people. They are going to kill you!"

He laughed and told her, "You are a very frightened woman. The agreement was decided by the elders. Everything is good now. My two daughters are going to go to their house someday. What was done in the past is now forgiven. There will be no problem for my family now."

Zarka appealed to him not to trust the Didars. "You compromised your daughters' lives and you lost all the money you had, but you still owe them more."

"I have the rest of the money," he announced. "I will take it to them in two days. I am sure my daughters will have a good life. This was the elders' wise decision. I did not want to give my daughters to the Didar family. I had no choice because I was afraid that they would take revenge on my brothers, children and cousins if I didn't agree. There will be someone to make sure my daughters are treated well. I would never have just given my daughters over to that family and let that be that. They have a father, and I will never let anyone hurt my daughters. I accepted the agreement because there was no other way to end the feud."

He called me, "Come here, my big nephew. This nephew will ask about my daughters. He will take care of them. I am proud of him." I smiled, but I wasn't feeling very well. "Is everything okay?" he asked.

"I am fine," I said, "but my head hurts a little bit."

"Oh, I must buy your medication," he said. "Just wait until Friday. I wanted to go this week but I was occupied with many affairs. I have to give the final payment to Didars. I have a meeting with them. I will leave for your medication on Friday. Please don't eat oily food. Drink only clean water, and do not make yourself too tired. Take the medication that you have from before."

"I gave my medication to Latifa."

"What are you talking about? You shouldn't have done that. You were supposed to take all of it."

"I am sorry I gave it away. I was trying to help her."

"Don't you worry," he said. "I will buy your medication soon. Go with Zarka when she returns to her home. Stay a few days. But before I go on Friday, come back, and see me. I will be worried about you. If you are sick, I will take you with me to the hospital in Khost."

137

Chapter 8

Now my aunt was ready to return to her husband. The week had flown by. The whole family did not want her to go back. She took care of everything for us. She gave me a bag with her clothes and went out the gate. It was a two-hour trip to her house on foot. My headache came back. It was getting worse every hour. The fever returned, too, but I was still excited to be going to my aunt's house. She had a huge garden with many kinds of fruit.

Mansour Baba's shrine was not far off our path, and my aunt said, "You must go there. It is a good shrine. People drive from many different states for months to visit it."

"Aunt, I am so tired of shrines" I said. "Please."

"Don't say this!" she admonished. "It is sinful. He will follow you, and come to your house at midnight."

I was so afraid. I immediately turned in the direction of the shrine and said, "Aunt, let's go to his grave. I will not say anything bad."

It took us about 20 minutes to walk to the shrine. In the middle of nowhere we saw the huge monument with all sorts of different colored blankets covering the grave. Mansour Baba was famous for his courage. Some people were waiting outside. There were three caretakers with brooms in their hands, and they touched people with these brooms. They waved their brooms across my head. I was given the usual ashes and salt. We left the grave and got home by the afternoon.

The excitement I'd had was gone. I was so sick. I needed to lie down. My aunt put blankets over me to keep me warm. I had chills and a bad headache and I was vomiting. The whole family was worried. That night Mansour Baba came to my dream. I was so afraid. The next morning, I was not able to walk. My aunt's husband Fareed said, "I will help you to get home."

We walked slowly. Sometimes, he held me in his arms and sometimes on his back. It took three or more hours to get there. I was counting the moments until I reached Uncle Shar Khan, and we would get to a doctor. We had almost made it to Uncle Shar Khan's house when we heard the sound of the bullets, fifteen or twenty shots. After a death in the village, other families do not celebrate their happiness for many months, so I was a little shocked.

As we got closer to Uncle Shar Khan's house we saw villagers running toward it. Fareed asked one of them, "What happened? Who was shooting?" The man, out of breath, said, "Somebody shot Shar Khan!"

When I heard these words, I jumped from Fareed's arms and began run to Uncle Shar Khan's house. Off on the right at the bottom of the hill, there was a woman screaming, and two of his brothers were running in that direction. I followed in that direction to Uncle Shar Khan's fields. When I got there, I saw Uncle Shar Khan on the ground, his white clothes full of blood. He was hit many times. Blood was coming from his hand where a bullet had pierced through. The old woman tore a piece of her scarf and wrapped it under his chin, then she tied his feet. His eyes were closed, and I just stood by his head. I realized that my Aunt Fatima and Aunt Zarka were right — Uncle Shar Khan had made the wrong decision. He sacrificed himself and his two daughters.

They took the dead body to the house. All the villagers came. They were running from all different sides of the village. In no time, the fields were full. A huge crowd gathered. I was pushed further and further back. I was not able to see his face anymore. The sorrow was imprinted on my brain forever.

Fareed told me, "Let's take you home to get a little rest. I will come back here."

"No, I want to stay here with him."

"No, you have to leave immediately. You will get sicker if you stay." He clutched my arm and lifted me on to his shoulders. He brought me to Uncle Dawood's house. My grandmother was preparing herself to go to Uncle Shar Khan's house. She was talking aloud, "Shar Khan, I told you, do not give away your daughters! I told you not to deal with those people! This is the result. He lost his life. He lost his money, and his daughters' lives are destroyed. Nobody will marry them all their lives. The girls will never have husbands. They have no future."

"What will happen to the girls?" I asked. "And the money?"

"Those people were very sneaky," she said. "They tricked Uncle Shar Khan. They showed their anger. They showed that they did not forgive his family. First of all, they made the whole family very poor and weak. Shar Khan sold all his trees. All his profit was given to that family. Then, they took three million rupees. Second, they got his two daughters. They made them bound to their family for life. Those girls will wait for this family forever, and nobody will dare to marry them. If anyone tries to marry either one of them, Didar's family will interfere and stop the wedding from happening. Nobody wants to get involved with such a dangerous family. Third, Uncle Shar Khan is killed. He was the head of the family. They wanted to kill the most important person, and that is the person that leads the family. It would have been better not to deal with these people at all."

Grandmother abruptly turned around, adjusted her scarf and left for Uncle Shar Khan's to pay her respects. I was left behind.

Fareed knew of an Afghani family, the Akbars, that had been living in Pakistan and would be returning there soon. Fareed and my uncle decided to send me with them; three of my maternal mother's side lived there. But before I went there, I had to wait for four long days, fighting the fever and other symptoms of malaria. And of course I was very upset about Uncle Shar Khan's death.

To comfort me, my grandmother told me even though he was dead, he was still alive. She explained that he was watching over me. She added that if I went to his grave he could hear me.

On the day before I was to leave for Pakistan, my cousin Leila took me to see Uncle Shar Khan's grave and to find the prescription for the malaria medicine that had never been filled. We saw his wife who was fetching water from the well. She asked me if we wanted to go into her house, so I did. I saw the pistol, Uncle Shar Khan's pistol, hanging on the wall close to a picture of him. His rifle was leaning in a corner of the room. I hated the sight of them. Uncle Shar Khan was killed by the same kind of weapons.

His family gave me the prescription. From there I decided to go to his grave and pray for him and thank him for all the help. I wished he had gone to Khost the week before. I just sat near his grave for thirty minutes. I felt like he was sitting near me. Before I left, I said good bye and thanked him again for everything. Then, Leila and I returned home.

The evening before I was leaving for Pakistan, the family gathered one last time. I asked Uncle Dawood if I could go to Latifa's grave to tell her how sorry I was that I was unable to get to her on time to help her. Uncle Dawood said her grave was much too far away and that Latifa would be so disappointed in me if I somehow wasn't back in time for my trip to Pakistan.

"You should go to Pakistan," Uncle Dawood said. "You will get better there. I will talk to your parents to let them know that you are there in Pakistan because of your sickness. You can live with your uncles in Pakistan. They will take care of everything."

Then he thanked me for helping his baby Baryalai survive and for taking care of the sheep all this time. I said goodbye to my grandmother. I said good bye to my cousins and uncle. Then Uncle Dawood took me to the Akbar residence because they were leaving the next morning.

The Akbars tried to put me at ease from the start. They told me, "We will take you to Pakistan tomorrow. You will find good doctors, and you will get better soon after that." I was excited. I had heard a lot about life in Pakistan. I believed that people there had better lives than in my village. I asked about where we were going. "Would people there speak Dari, Pashto, Urdu, or Farsi?"

"Pashto," I was told. Most of the population there is Pashtun and they have lived there forever." That was all the information I got.

As I closed my eyes, I imagined I was going to a beautiful place where there would be schools and homes that I knew from Kabul. In conversations I had heard that Pakistan was a great country. People had electricity, beautiful houses and great schools. People had a different lifestyle from the village. Fighting sleep, I thought about what I was wearing. The shirt had a torn front pocket. The side was ripped to my waist. I thought if I had a little bit better clothes, people would not look at me or judge me. I fell asleep.

Chapter 9

Early the next morning, the whole family and I started the trip to Pakistan in an old Toyota station wagon. We had to push it down the road to get it to start. On our way, the family was very nice to me. They bought me food and drinks. After a long drive, I noticed that we were traveling on real concrete roads, not like the dirt road in my village. By evening, I saw some electrical lights around the area. It was totally different from my village. After fifteen hours we crossed the border into Pakistan, and eventually arrived at the Akbars' residence.

There must have been thirty people, family mostly, there to greet us. The older children and adults welcomed me, but the young kids my age looked at me as if I were from a far-away land. At first, I thought their language was different, but, then, I realized they were speaking Pashto but with an accent I'd never heard.

"Are you Muslim?" they asked.

"Yes," I said.

"You talk funny."

"Well, I am from Kabul. We spoke Dari there."

"Do you and your parents pray?"

"Yes," I said, nodding. "They pray. I always saw them."

"Do you know how to pray?"

"Not very well," I admitted. "I was living in a village and no one taught me there. People there start praying at the age of seven or eight."

"Maybe you are not Muslim," one of them said. "You are not seven? Why don't you know how to pray yet?"

"I bet your parents are *kafir*," said another. "We learned at school that people who did not leave during the Russian regime are all communists and *kafir*. People like that do not pray at all. They dress shamefully! We learned all about you at school."

"Yeah!" said another. "And we learned that for those who don't follow Islamic law, we should do *jihad* and kill the person and the whole family. We can enter heaven easily just by killing one *kafir*. We will show you."

They began pushing me a little, arguing with me, and one of them said, "We are going to find a gun or a knife to kill you tonight."

I was so afraid that I did not sleep the whole night. I was counting the minutes until they would come to kill me. If I heard a person go to the bathroom, I guessed that it was someone coming to kill me now. I kept the blanket very tight around my body and prayed, "Please, God, help me. Please watch over me. It's not my fault that I did not learn how to pray. Maybe it was the war and fighting. There was no time for my family to teach me how to be Muslim. Anyway, not that I could remember."

I felt feverish all this time and I wondered if I had forgotten what they taught me. Here I was in my new situation, but it seemed very familiar to me. All the kids were already judging me and calling me *kafir*. I had heard that name many times before but I still did not know the meaning.

The next morning, I asked the family, "Please take me to my uncle's house. I have never met them before."

There were hundreds of thoughts in my brain. How are they planning to treat me when they find out I am here? I was only going to be here that one night, so it didn't matter so much how I was treated. But with my uncle's family, I would live with them forever.

When it was time for me to go, a man about my own father's age, Satar, took me to uncle's house by bus. We had to jump on quickly because it didn't stop for us. There were people on the top of the bus, too. All the windows were open. It was covered in decorations of bright green and yellow. Religious writings adorned the inside walls, too. There was one seat open next to a woman covered in a burka, and I tried to sit there. I was pushed away by a man nearby who scolded me, "You cannot sit next to a woman!"

I stood and leaned against a pole until we reached our

stop. Their village was not too far. It was about twenty minutes further on foot. We got to the small town, which had maybe about thirty shops total, and my guardian showed me my uncle's village. "We are going over there to that place," he said, pointing to barren grey hills covered with houses that were surrounded by walls about five feet high, just tall enough to keep the women out of sight.

We walked up one hill and down it to the next. The houses were very close to each other, made of stones held together with clay. They looked temporary; the walls were weak. Curtains were substitutes for doors, and round holes served as windows. We walked through the woods to the next hill. Dogs chased after us. When we finally reached my uncle's house, three aunts came running to me, smiling. Their dresses were very full and reached to the ground. They wore long full sleeves with a bodice. They hugged me and kissed my cheeks, then took us to their compound.

They started to prepare food for us, but Satar told them that I was very sick and I was not allowed to eat oily food because of the malaria.

We sat outside the house. There were three cows, two with calves, in front of us, and so many dogs. Neighbors from other houses stared at me, commenting to each other, "This guy came from Kabul." They were staring. Uncle Manan arrived,

148

walking with a cane. He had a noticeable limp. He hugged me and said he was happy that I was there. He saw that I did not feel very well, and said that after lunch and afternoon prayers, we would go to the doctor.

At prayer time, I told them, "I do not know how to pray." Uncle Manan frowned, and I understood I said something wrong. He told me not to repeat that to anyone, and once we returned from the doctor he would teach me how to pray.

The doctor did not seem like a doctor to me. He was wearing a white prayer cap. He asked me many questions. "You came from Kabul? Hmmm. Who is your prophet? Do you believe in God? How many times do you pray in a day?" I looked to my uncle for help. I pretended to be shy to avoid having to answer him. I had a fever and headache, I just wanted to go somewhere to sleep and have some rest. But his questions did not stop. Some of them were about my family, my dad, my mother, and my sister. Finally, he checked my blood.

"You have malaria," he said. "I will give you medication, and you will be fine."

When we returned to his compound, Uncle Manan gave me some medication, but it did not help me at all. I was getting worse and worse. Everyone there said, "It takes time. You should wait. It will work for you later."

Five days passed and I felt as bad as I had back in Mangal. I was too weak to walk. My uncle decided it was time to take me to a different doctor.

Very often these so-called doctors had really only been trained as medical assistants during the time of the Russian regime and Mujahidin. They opened small clinics where they sold medication and offered simple remedies, pills like ibuprofen and aspirin. However, the second doctor my uncle took me to was a little better. He did not ask any questions. He drew some blood and confirmed that I had malaria. He gave me drops and medication. I took this medication for two weeks and got much better.

Then my uncle put me to work. He had difficulty walking, and his own children and nephews were much too young to do much of the work. I was the only person that could help my uncle now by taking care of the livestock. The only difference between my village and Pakistan was the animals I watched. Instead of sheep, I minded cows.

The children from the village were always singing religious songs. All the songs were about jihad and critical of the Russian communist regime that was in power in Afghanistan at the time. Their families encouraged their singing.

A couple of times, my uncle sent me with other village children to show me how to take care of the animals. I still had a lot of problems with the village children. I had no idea how they knew about me, that I came from Kabul, but they did, and their language was totally different from my village dialect. They were friendly with each other, but, when I appeared, everyone became quiet. They asked me questions about Islam. They told me the same thing that I had heard from the family in Pakistan when I first arrived. I heard the same questions. Their beliefs were the same, too.

They taunted me, "You did not immigrate to this country when we did. We came here to keep our religion from non-Muslims that attacked our country. It is called *hegrat*. But you and your family did not. You lived with those infidels when the Russian regime started. Your family did not do *jihad*. That means that you and your family are *kafir*."

I was trying to persuade them that we weren't infidels and we were Muslim, but it was so difficult to talk with them. They wouldn't discuss anything, they just repeated the same things they had learned from their families and at school. They were taught that non-Muslims are our enemies and that it is part of the religion to kill nonbelievers. They also believed that anyone who did not emigrate during that time must be communist and non-Muslim. Killing anyone like that was a direct route to heaven.

No one played with me or talked with me. I tried to make friends, to start conversations, but no one was open to being my friend. Their older family members told them that my family and I were communists and not Muslims. At that time, I did not understand the meaning of "communism," "non-Muslim," and "hegrat." Before I got to Pakistan, I had never thought that I would encounter such a situation. I wished I could go to school, where I might meet different people. Maybe I'd even meet another true friend like Ismail.

My uncle never thought about my education, but a couple of months later, he got a letter from my dad. My father had learned that I had come to Pakistan. In his letter he expressed his concern about his son's education, and told Uncle Manan to send me to school. "I know he is very behind," he wrote, "but I am sure you can help him in his education." My uncle reluctantly agreed.

Uncle Manan warned me not to tell anyone where I was from. He told me I could not introduce myself the usual way I had learned in Afghanistan. Back there everyone asked you who your father was, and whatever his position was came before your name. He told me to say only that I was Manan's nephew.

Uncle Manan walked me to the school for admission. The school was located about twenty minutes from my new home, close to a small town. We approached fifteen khaki-colored canvas tents and a huge crowd. Religious songs were coming to my ears. Children were running back and forth and sneaking like little mice from underneath the sides of the tents. Their hair and lips were oily and their faces were dry from sliding through the dusty ground.

My uncle pointed and said, "This is your school."

I thought we had come upon some travelers who were staying there temporarily. This was a school?

I heard a whole class repeating a religious verse. They chanted in unison what their teacher told them to say. He called out for them to say it with more feeling, and they repeated it with greater volume and passion. Then I saw a teacher beating a boy's palms with a switch. Every time the boy pulled his hands away, the teacher hollered, "Three more!"

We continued to the principal's office, which was a huge tent. There were no table or chairs; the principal sat on a mat on the ground, drinking tea with some teachers. He said hello to my uncle. My Uncle Manan asked the principal to admit me in the school.

The principal looked at me and asked, "Is he your nephew?"

"Yes, yes." He did not offer any detail.

With a switch in his hand, he pointed to me, "What is your name?"

I told him my name.

He asked, "Where did you come from?"

"I came from Kabul."

He said, "You came from Kabul? From the communist city? What about your family?"

"They are not here."

"You must know how to speak Dari because I know that you do not speak Pashto very well," he said with a sarcastic tone.

"Yes, I can speak Dari."

"Okay, I will show you to your class."

He took me directly to the class. It was a second grade class because of my age. There were fifty boys in one tent. The floor was dusty because the carpet was very thin. I sat in the back. The teacher, who wore a big brown turban, was teaching something I did not understand at all. He was talking about *jihad*.

I was completely confused. I had never heard of *jihad*, and I did not know what it was supposed to mean. I wondered if it was kind of sickness, or some kind of a car. All the students in the class were reading the writing aloud. They spoke at the tops of their voices. I also read, from the book of the boy next to me, but with great difficulty. This was a second grader reader, and I had never finished first grade.

The class ended and the teacher left. The students began talking, playing and pushing each other. I noticed that all the boys were wearing prayer caps, some blue, some white, some with designs. I stuck out like a sore thumb with my bare head. A classmate asked me where I was from. I answered, "I came from Kabul."

Now almost everyone seemed to gather around me. They were asking questions and staring at me. They asked me, "Do you know about your religion? Who is your prophet? Where is your family? Why can't you speak Pashto very well? We heard that people in Kabul are *kafir!*" They began pushing me and making fun of me. Some of the boys took off their caps and put them on my head. They called me bad names, and they said my family was *kafir*. "We will do jihad with you and your family," they said. "Why did you come here?"

A boy pulled my hair. Another one put a cap back on my head. I remembered my uncle's warning to remain quiet, so in spite of all the teasing and bullying, I made no attempt to fight back. All I could do was wait for the day to end. Finally, a school bell announced the end of the class day, and all the boys, one after another, slapped the top of my head and told me to get out as they took off for their homes. I was the only boy left. I sat cross-legged on the floor, wondering how I would get out of this predicament.

The next day, I entered the classroom looking for a seat, but nobody let me sit next to them. I tried to sit in the back row, but the boy there pushed me away. I left that row and chose a different place. The students there did the same thing with me. The group made fun of me as they pushed me again and again. Finally, the teacher came to the class, and he found a place for me to sit, close to the back door of the tent, separate from the other students.

First, we learned arithmetic. We did subtraction and multiplication. It was hard for me, but I understood a little about the math. Later, another teacher came in. Everybody took out their books — very broken books. Some had to share. When a student couldn't answer a question, he was hit with a switch. The teacher asked me where my book was. I told him I didn't know because I hadn't gotten any books. The students began to laugh. The teacher warned me to bring my books by the next day.

The teacher asked another boy what the topic was the day before and he called out, "*Jihad.*" Suddenly I grasped that this new word had something to do with fighting or beating someone. Next, the teacher introduced the new topic of the day by telling the students top open their books to the next page. At the top it read "G — Gun." And beneath that, sentences like, "My father has a gun at home. The gun has thirty bullets. We kill *kafirs* with the guns." Later I would learn that these books came from the Pakistani government and were designed to indoctrinate us.

The teacher pointed row by row to instruct the students to read each sentence. He started with the students who sat in the back. I was the third person to read. I had trouble sounding out the words in my sentence. When I stopped somewhere or made a mistake, my classmates on my right and left, at the teacher's command, slapped me in the face. If one didn't slap me soundly enough, the teacher told the other one to hit me again. When the teacher wasn't satisfied with the quality of their slaps, he called them to come to the front of the room. He said he would show them what a proper slap was. He slapped their faces, and he told them, "Go back and do the same."

On my way home that day my face was still numb and swollen. I stopped at a river stream to wash my face and feel the cool water on my stinging cheeks.

The next day, the students were excited about class we were going to have because everyone liked the teacher. They talked about how much fun he was. When he arrived he smiled and said, in Pashto, of course, "Today the lesson I have planned for you is to have you show me everything you know about all living creatures. Listen to the directions. I'm going to say the name of a creature. Raise your hand if the creature I mention flies. If it doesn't fly, then do not raise your hand." So far, so good. I understood him. He continued explaining, "If someone makes a mistake, there will be a punishment for that student."

First, he said, "*Kargh* (crow)." I didn't recognize this word. The whole class raised their hands, but I had hesitated before deciding. Before I had my arm fully extended, the teacher pointed at me and directed everyone to create an aisle in the middle of the class. "First, you are going to give your neighbor on the right and then your neighbor on the left a piggy-back ride from one end of the classroom all the way to the other end," he said to me.

They were older and bigger than me, but I did as I was instructed. They were so heavy, but somehow I did it. After that, I began to get nervous. I knew myself. I knew that when I became nervous, I made more mistakes.

"*Bizo* (monkey)," the instructor said next, and nobody raised their hands but me. Looking at me, the teacher announced, "You might be a little too tired to carry the boys again, so maybe you would prefer to do another punishment. Four slaps from your neighbor on the right and then from your left. You must choose."

All the children started shouting out one choice or another, but I could not understand and I became confused. I stood between the two boys and politely chirped, "Yes. Yes." It was the easiest word that I knew. The first boy slapped my face. "One!" shouted the boys. "Two! Three! Four!" Then the second boy took his turn as everyone counted as loud as they could.

On the next word, I did not make a mistake. With the fourth word, I made a mistake again. The teacher told the students, "It's your turn, class. You can decide which punishment we will give him."

A boy took one of his slippers from his foot and put its tip in my mouth. He said I had to keep it in my mouth and balance on one foot for two minutes. Thankfully, it was noon, and the "tak, tak, tak" sound that always announced dismissal came, and I was able to escape for the day.

Day by day I was going home by myself, already worrying about the next day. None of my classmates wanted to walk with me. If I attempted to join them, they called out, "*Kafir, kafir!*" I was so lonely.

Chapter 10

My peers knew so much more about religion than me. They learned about religion from their families, in the mosques, and in school. It began in their first year of school and continued in every grade six days a week. At my school in Kabul, we had studied numbers, reading, handwriting, spelling, and so on. Did we even study the Koran? It seemed such a long time ago. I couldn't remember.

One of my teachers lived in the same village where I lived with my uncle, and he advised Uncle Manan to show me how to pray and to help me to practice. Uncle Manan took me to the pasture on a hill where I usually took the livestock. Along the way, he stopped to cut several sticks. I asked what he was doing and he told me, "I am going to show you how to pray."

My uncle showed me how to stand and to read a verse. I did not understand what I was reading at all. It was in Arabic. Any little mistake was answered with a swift hit to my back with the sticks. That was the first lesson.

Uncle decided that I had to read a prayer and memorize it until I was able to say it by heart. Then he would assign another part for me to memorize. If I hesitated, he beat me. If I mispronounced a word, he beat me. If I lost my concentration, he beat me. Every day after the beatings, he asked questions about the prayers that I had just learned. I responded in Arabic, but I did not know the meaning of what I was saying.

After three or four months, I was ready to learn the physical side of the prayers. He had switches for these sessions, too. He told me what to do first and what to do next. I read my prayer loudly. I made many mistakes trying to put the words with the actions. When I made a mistake, huge or very small, I was struck on my shoulders and my butt. With all the beatings, my interest in the prayers totally disappeared. We said the same words every single day five times a day, but I did not know what I was saying. I thought if the prayer was for God, a person should understand what the words meant, what they wanted from God, and what the purpose of the prayer was. I had none of that in my experience.

The rules at the school required that all students came to the center of the tents to sing religious songs to begin each morning. Most of the songs were about mujahidin, Islam, and *jihad*. At the end of the songs, the teachers of each class took attendance and called the names of each student. If someone had been absent in the previous class, the teacher beat the students on the palms of their hands in the front of all the students in the school. The sticks they used were very thick.

161

When the teachers hit a student, his hands were red and hurt for many days. The punishment for students who were absent for more than one day was having their feet beaten with three or four sticks held together.

There were other kinds of punishment, too. For example, a teacher would put a pen between each of the student's fingers, then squeeze his hands for one minute. That was very painful. I had extensive experience with every kind of punishment they used. So even when I had a recurrence of malaria, I continued attending school because I was so afraid of the punishment. Despite the fever and headaches, I kept going. I was not able to pay much attention to the teacher because of my condition, and sometimes I became dizzy and lost consciousness for seconds at a time. My teachers repeatedly told the students on my right or left to slap me hard across the face if they caught me. They kept doing this to me, and one day after all the beatings and slaps I'd already received that week, I received a slap that knocked me out of my seat. The slap was so hard that my nose started bleeding, and I passed out. The classmate and the teacher brought some water and they poured it in my face. The teacher told me, "When you feel strong enough, go home."

My aunts met me as I came into the compound. I had tears in my eyes and blood stains on my clothes. Making no mention of the physical abuse I'd been withstanding, I complained that I was very sick.

My aunts shared good news. "We do not know exactly when yet, but your Uncle Amanullah, his wife Aisha, his three daughters, and two sons are immigrating to here from Afghanistan."

His oldest son Hamid was getting his bachelor's degree, and his second son Abdul Satar was a mechanic, my aunts explained. The oldest daughter Brishna had graduated from high school, and the second daughter, Aruzo, had finished tenth grade. Youngest daughter Maryam, who was about six years old, was ready to start school.

On the one hand, it was good news to me that they were coming, but on the other hand, I was a little concerned. I knew people in this area would not welcome them because the whole community here believed that my family was communist and non-Muslim. But what could I do? Nobody would listen to a small kid like me, so I did not share my fears. Instead, like everyone else in the family I waited for their arrival, and, one evening, the news that my uncle and his family had arrived in my village came.

At the time, I did not know that my uncle was bringing his family to escape from the fighting in Kabul. The Russian regime had fallen and was being replaced by the Mujahidin.

At first, no one in the family recognized me. We had not seen each other for two years. My appearance now was so different from when I had last seen them, and I no longer looked like a little boy from Kabul. To them, I looked like a village boy, complete with a prayer cap.

I told my cousins stories about everything that had happened since I left Kabul. I embraced my new identity, for the moment, and spoke my new language, Pashto, just to show off a little bit to them. I was so delighted about my family and my cute cousin Maryam that I totally forgot about how bad I felt. I told them about Uncle Shar Khan, Aunt Fatima, Latifa, and all the events that I had witnessed in Mangal. I did not want to make them sad about the village. They had just moved there, and they did not know how the people around us viewed our family. They did not know what was in store for them. My cousins had not gone to religious schools, yet they knew how to pray, read and write, and they were smart enough.

Amanullah's family saw that I was very sick and noticed that even walking exhausted me. In the middle of the night I woke and vomited a couple of times. I had a high fever and a severe headache. The family understood that I was very sick. My Uncle Amanullah took me to a good doctor. On the way to the doctor, he asked me, "How is school? How are the people and students? How are they treating you?"

I said, "It is okay."

When he looked at my face, he understood that I was not telling him the truth. He coaxed me a little with his soft words and gentle manner. "I am your uncle. You must tell me everything. I brought my family here because of the war. I want to protect my family and that includes you. Your education is important to your family and to me. You have got to be honest with me. Are you happy?"

The sadness in my life, losing my aunt and Uncle Shar Khan, all the problems in school, the beatings, the slaps, the teasing and name-calling all came rushing to my mind. I was trying to be strong, but all these issues made me very emotionally weak, and my uncle saw the tears in my eyes. I told him, "I am not going to that school anymore. It is very difficult to be in this school. I do not know a lot of the religious teachings they talk about. It is better to take me to a different school."

When we arrived at the doctor's location, I showed him the prescription that I had taken from Uncle Shar Khan. This doctor said, "You should have seen a doctor six months ago because you did not take all the necessary medication." He gave me the correct medicine. I took it, and finally the malaria was gone forever.

My cousins were educated, but my Uncle Amanullah was not. He was a military person. Although he was strict, he was an open-minded person. He loved to connect the family and keep the members together. In our culture, keeping the family together is important because it makes them more powerful. Marrying cousins was a good way to unite and strengthen families. It was a very important goal for him.

But my uncle's family's experience in the village was like mine. Their clothes, their lifestyle, and language were totally different from the clothes, lifestyle, and language of the people who lived in that village. They, villagers, were all very religious. I remember one particular time when very close family members refused to come to my uncle's house because they believed Uncle Amanullah's family was *kafir*. People asked Amanullah a lot of questions and argued with him for no reason. Sometimes verbal arguments developed into physical altercations. Frequently, the villagers treated my family members disrespectfully.

In spite of the turmoil, Uncle Amanullah attempted to be civil with everyone. We had to live among these people. At that time, my Uncle Amanullah had no money, and we stayed there because it was affordable. There were no bills to pay, and uncle was able to build temporary housing to keep the family safe.

Amanullah's daughters' lives changed radically. It was a difficult adjustment for them. They missed all the freedom they had had in Afghanistan. They missed their lives, their schools and their friends. There was no joy in this place for them. My cousins had left their schools and colleges when they came and had hoped to start school here, but there was no school for women. In fact, they could not leave the house much at all. Even when they went to the doctor, a male family member was required to accompany them. And they had to wear *kamis*, long, heavy dresses made of yards of material that were loose fitting with long sleeves, and over them they wore *chadors*, which covered them from head to toe. They had to keep their faces covered, too. All of this was new to my cousins.

Fetching water was the other approved excursion for girls in the village. They were expected to transport the water in big clay pots on their heads. When they went, they had the same problem with the women from the village that Uncle Amanullah and I experienced. Village women said things such as, "You are members of the communist family." The women and girls criticized them about everything. They asked impertinent questions, "Why don't you know how to pray? How did you go to school? Why don't you pray in Kabul? Why don't the women cover? Why aren't they modest?"

Compared to the adults and the older children, my cousin Maryam and I were less affected. We were relatively happy, and I was glad to finally have a playmate.

Chapter 11

Sometime soon after my uncle settled here, there was more good news. Some of the villagers, along with my uncle, tried to establish a school in the village. After contacting many different agencies and going through the usual red tape, the International Rescue Committee (IRC) agreed to provide tents to house the school. Gathering supplies and other preparations for the school took several months. My uncle gathered blackboards, books and chalk for forty students.

Now, we just needed a teacher. My uncle had no teaching experience, so he was not a viable candidate. The mullah was a little more educated. But after reviewing the mullah's educational background, a visiting IRC agent decided to limit the village to only one tent, for first, second and third grades, because the mullah was not qualified to teach higher grades. Approval for the school was finally given and it was ready to open.

My uncle encouraged villagers to send their children to this new school and permit them to study together. Nobody listened to my uncle, so he persuaded the mullah to tell everyone in his mosque that all the children ought to come to school and learn. At the very least, they could learn about their religion. Still people did not come because they knew the idea had originated with my uncle. The positive news was that my uncle told Maryam and me to attend the school. We were the first two people that were admitted. A couple days later, my Uncle Manan brought his four kids to the school.

The villagers watched and day by day, more students joined us. Some of the villagers even began to send their daughters. Within a couple of months there were forty-five students and the tent was over capacity. The boys sat on the right side of the tent, and the girls sat on the left.

There was no opportunity for my older cousins Brishna and Aruzo to continue with their studies, but they remained hopeful and helped Maryam and me with our school subjects. Maryam and I studied very hard. We were always the first in the class. We earned the highest grades, too. Maryam was a better learner than I was, but because she was a female, the teacher put me first in the class. Whoever was first in the class had more responsibilities. I was responsible for laying out the rug and bringing the chalk to the classroom.

We loved school, but the small village kids kept asking annoying questions about our family and religion. Our cousins always encouraged us to ignore the other kids and not get into fights with them. "You are the first in the class, and you know more than other students," the said. "Try to be polite to them. Always help them. That will change their point of view. They will be nice to you." They were right. Within six months, all the children stopped taunting us with all those questions. The whole village knew that we were helping their kids with their studies. They were becoming more tolerant and respectful of us, but of course, their religious views didn't budge.

The subjects at the school were the same as in my previous school. Aruzo and Brishna were trying to help our neighbors with reading and writing. They often recounted their experiences from the past with them, and they enjoyed hearing about their schools, TVs and the house they had lived in. The village girls were very interested in their stories. That was the only way to deal with people and change their minds and ideas a little.

Hamid, Maryam's oldest brother, was twenty-eight years old, but he was still single. The family economic situation had become a little better because my Uncle Amanullah had opened a store nearby. However, it was not enough to cover all the needs of the family. Hamid went to a different country to earn some money. In the meantime, Amanullah was trying to find a suitable wife for Hamid. Normally, people in my village got married by the time they reached twenty-five years old.

Another uncle of mine, Uncle Shawali, had five daughters. He lived in Afghanistan on the border with Iran; it took about three days to travel to that state. Amanullah sometimes traveled to meet with his brother, and, for the most part, Amanullah was happy with his nieces. All of them were young, ranging from twenty to twenty-five. Amanullah was very interested in choosing a wife for Hamid from among those girls. He was trying to keep the family together and did not want to lose his nieces by having them marry outside the family. It was the topic of discussion in our family every day. Specifically, he was interested in arranging a match between Hamid and his niece Rahima. Most of the family disagreed with my uncle's choice. However, as was the tradition, he was the head of the family, and he made all the decisions for his family. After a long time deliberating, he planned to go to his brother's house.

He returned after three weeks with the traditional chocolate and gifts to celebrate an engagement. He announced, "I've arranged Hamid's engagement to Rahima."

The whole family celebrated. I had not seen any happiness in my uncle's house until this, and Maryam and I laughed and celebrated the good news along with everyone else. There was music and singing until midnight. Maryam was asleep but I was still awake, watching and listening from our room, when my uncle shared the details. One of his daughters, he said, would marry one of Shawali's sons.

I looked at my Aunt Aisha's eyes, and her daughters Aruzo and Brishna's eyes. At first, I thought that they were crying because they were so happy, but I guessed wrong. They screamed at Amanullah, "Why did you do this?" Aisha reminded him that she'd said, "I told you whatever your brother wants, just give it to him but not your daughter."

I thought my uncle had promised Aruzo to one of Shawali's sons. She was the oldest, and smart. However, as the conversation progressed, I began to realize that they were referring to Maryam. I was stunned! I crept closer and listened to their argument to understand what had happened.

"How could you promise them Maryam? She is not even eight years old. You've just totally destroyed her life. She is only in second grade. Look at the success she's had in school. You are taking her from school and giving her to that family? Who knows what her dreams are for the future?" Other relatives joined the conversation and the argument became more heated. I feared Maryam might wake up and hear the terrible discussion between the family members. I closed the door very slowly, which they must have heard because they stopped their conversation. They thought that Maryam had woken up. Everything was quiet.

I returned to my room and looked at Maryam. She was sleeping soundly. I imagined she was dreaming about her future and the plans that we had been making every day. Every day I told her, "I will be a doctor, and you will be my nurse." She always retorted, "What are you talking about? I will be a doctor, and you will be my nurse! I am smarter than you." Jokingly, she sometimes stated, "If I ask you a question and you can answer it, then you can be the doctor, and I will be your nurse." God had blessed her with an extremely advanced intellect and desire to learn. She was always asking new questions, and I was not able to answer most of them. I had to repeatedly respond, "Okay, okay. I will be your nurse." Now that I knew the true plans for her future, I could not sleep at all. I cried because I did not want to lose Maryam or the future we planned together.

The next morning, the whole family was quiet and sad. No one wanted to tell Maryam what had happened. Suspecting nothing, she was still happy and excited. "Let's go to school," she said. "When we come back, we'll sing. A lot of people will come. The whole village will come. We will ask our teacher to excuse us from classes for a couple of days, and all our classmates will come to our home with their parents."

She caught the dejected look on my face. "What's wrong?" she asked.

"Nothing," I said. Aruzo and Brishna had told me not to

tell Maryam.

Even though they were keeping the news from Maryam, it was an important part of the tradition to tell all the people in the village of the engagements. As news spread, people visited our house with congratulations. Maryam's mother pleaded with the guests, "Please, do not tell your children that Maryam is engaged. If she hears the news, she will be upset. She won't be able to focus on school. It will be very sad news for her."

Everyone agreed to keep the secret, but besides being the smartest girl, Maryam was a very sensitive girl. She could read the feelings of her family from their faces. She searched everybody's eyes again and again. I kept trying to divert her attention, so she would not think about it.

After several days of celebrating, the guests and the villagers stopped coming to our house. Word had spread from one side of the village to the other. Only Maryam did not know of the engagement that had been made on her behalf.

One day I went to school ahead of her. I heard some students talking about Maryam's engagement. I begged the whole class, "Please, you know Maryam helps everyone here. She is very nice, quiet and respectful. Please do not mention her engagement. If she finds out from you, she will not come to school anymore. She will be distraught by the news."

They promised me, but they were only children and

very young ones at that. And it wasn't long before one of the little girls talked about it and Maryam discovered that she was engaged.

After school, Maryam and I usually walked home together with some of the other children. On the day Maryam found out, I was waiting in the front of the school tent for her, not knowing she had been told. Almost all the other students had already gone, and I was still waiting. It was not uncommon that she helped other students with their homework before we left. I waited for more than fifteen minutes. Finally, I went back into the classroom, and Maryam was sitting there by herself, crying.

I approached her thinking she was sick; often she suffered from asthma attacks. Since she was six months old, we had regularly taken her to the hospital. The doctors suggested keeping her in warm places. She loved oranges, but she never ate them because the doctors advised against it due to her asthma. Maryam got sick about every two weeks, depending on the weather. Sometimes she stayed in the hospital for several days at a time. The doctor had said, "Let us hope for a better future because we cannot say how long she will survive." She usually got sick when she went to school in the cold weather, and that day was very cold.

I asked, "Are you sick?"

"No," she said.

"What's wrong?"

"Something worse than one of my asthma attacks has happened to me. I would be glad to have an asthma attack if it were the worst to happen to me. My dream to be a doctor will never happen! Never!"

"Are you crazy? You will be a doctor, and I will be your nurse."

She sighed. "No."

After a pause, she explained. Marva, a girl from the village, always earned grades almost as good as Maryam's, and was jealous of Maryam's success. On that day, she told Maryam, "Even if you are getting excellent grades, you will not be able to continue. You're already engaged. You will have a husband and babies. Your education is finished."

"Let's go home," I said. "Don't listen to anyone. Are you crazy? If you are engaged, why didn't they tell you? Marva just wanted to upset you." But I was sure that Maryam had already guessed my words were not true because she was very smart.

She cried all the way home, then confronted her mother. "Mom, why did you do this to me?" It was quite unexpected for Maryam to ask that kind of question because she was a very quiet and extremely respectful girl.

Her mom answered with a question, "What are you taking about? You are not engaged."

"It's true, Mom. Marva told me."

"She just wanted to make you upset because she is so jealous of you." My aunt wanted to keep Maryam's attention on school. Later she went to Marva's house and told Marva's mother, "Maryam is crying today because your daughter told Maryam about the engagement. I am sure she will not be able to focus on her subjects in school anymore."

Marva's mother became upset, and she beat Marva badly. She ordered her, "You are going to go to Maryam, and tell her that you are sorry! Tell her you were teasing!"

Back at home, Maryam's mom cried, but not in front of Maryam. The whole family was miserable. Maryam was so sad that she did not even want to play with me. I still attempted to cheer her up, but that day and night ended full of despair.

The next day was a school day. Maryam was undecided whether to go to school or not. I waited at the front of the door with my backpack, but Maryam still did not come out. I went back to our room and pleaded with her, "Maryam, please let's go. Don't listen to anyone. Marva lied to you. She was jealous of your grades."

"If it isn't true, why didn't Marva ever try and tease me like this before? We have been studying together for two years.

178

Why didn't she tell me before?"

I attempted a different approach. I picked up her books and said, "Let's go."

She wondered, "Do you think this is a good idea? I am an engaged girl. I cannot sit with other girls. Do you think my parents promised me to that family because I am not a very healthy girl? Am I right? They are giving me to Azizullah because I am a very shy and quiet person."

I kept reassuring her. "No, no, you are the best. Quiet is the best. You are not unhealthy. Many people have asthma. You are not the only one. The doctor said this ought to be gone very soon. You are still a little girl. Please, let's just take your books and go to school."

She was wiping her eyes with her small scarf. She did not smile and was not excited like normal; she was usually overjoyed to go to school. Today the whole house was quiet. The family avoided her because they were crying for her but did not want her to know. I was the only person who did not cry or show my sorrow in front of her. I always smiled for her, even though I was more worried than anybody else in her family. She was my best studying partner. We always did our homework together. We always got the highest grades.

That day, we did not have any homework done. We would not get the highest scores. We would have zeroes. We walked to the entrance of our school. At the front door, Marva was standing with a very sad face. She came close to Maryam, and she started crying in front of her. She said, "I am so sorry. I apologize. You are not engaged."

Maryam was still unsure, but she said, "Don't worry." She picked out one of her best pencils from her bag and gave it to Marva. "You like this pink pencil, don't you?" she asked. Both of them smiled and took their seats.

Thank God, I thought. I felt relieved. The previous twenty-four hours had felt like a year. I was sure Maryam was searching for answers about what had happened and what would happen to her in the future. We continued going to school. We never talked about the engagement of her brother. Conversations on the topic stopped in her family, too.

Chapter 12

When we weren't at school, Maryam and I sometimes played with the village kids. We hung a swing in a tree, and there was always a crowd around it. After learning about the engagement, Maryam lost interested in playing. Our school grades were still high although Maryam was not studying as hard as she had been.

To keep Maryam happy, we started to listen to the radio, and we became very interested in it. The area where we lived did not have any electricity, phones, computers, TVs or Internet. Not many people even had a radio. Most people were not interested, and thought that listening to the radio was against their religion. Certainly they did not permit their children to listen. However, my uncle usually listened to the BBC News on the radio he kept with him. Sometimes when he was searching for other stations, he found one with stories for children. Maryam and I were interested in listening to the stories and learning something. We usually listened to AM stations. We received help from Ibrahim, a shopkeeper who lived close to our house. Like my uncle, he listened to the radio. He gave us some books, which he had received from various radio stations such as BBC News. Some were biographies. Others were stories about animals and had beautiful drawings.

These pictures were different images from what we had been exposed to and were fascinating in contrast to our school books, which were so boring. When Aruzo helped us with schoolwork, she commented that the topics in our schoolbooks were not interesting. The books Ibrahim gave us, on the other hand, shared various aspects of life. They were in two different languages: Farsi and Pashto. I was trying to learn Pashto better since I needed it to communicate with everyone in the area. The children's books we were reading did not espouse any particular religion. Besides reading books, we decided to listen to the radio by ourselves, but we were not supposed to touch Amanullah's radio. We had no money to buy a radio of our own.

One day, I asked my aunt, who had come to Pakistan fifteen years earlier, "Is there a radio Maryam and I can use?" I knew there was one because my uncles who had gone to work in a different country had one. It was the type that had a recorder and radio together. I had been dreaming of having one like that.

Pointing to a storage room, my aunt replied, "Yes. We have a very old radio. It is in that room, but why are you asking? You are not allowed to use the radio."

The room where she pointed was full of different abandoned, unused things. It was disorganized and dark.

Maryam and I made finding the radio our mission. We had an image of the radio in our heads, thinking that it would be a very nice and beautiful radio. We described it to each other, imagining it in different ways. She thought it would be a black radio, but I pictured it as a white, shiny, new radio. We searched the room every day but came out empty-handed. We looked in all the corners. There were a lot of heavy items like tables, chairs, big pots and bags with rice, beans, and corn. It was very hard to move them. We worked to push the bags and get to the radio. We were also afraid of snakes because the place where we were living had plenty of them. People often found dangerous snakes around their houses. If we brushed up against anything and it touched our bodies while we were searching in the storage room, we went running out thinking that it was a snake. It could have been a cable or a bag we'd jostled.

Finally, one Friday, we decided that we had to find the radio that day, no matter what. We went into the room and searched for two hours. Then, we came out and helped our family for half an hour, so no one became suspicious. Then, we ran back inside the room. We worked like this for the whole day. Frustrated, we tried to organize the room back the way it had been, so nobody would be complaining. I pushed aside a plastic bag that I had moved many times in our search, and a battery dropped out. Maryam stopped me, "Open the bag. Look at this battery." I picked up the bag and another battery came out. I quickly set it down, opened it and, lo and behold, there it was!

The radio was not white or black. The casing was cracked and dirty. Nonetheless, we grabbed it and ran to our study room. We had so much work to do! We used towels to clean the inside. The battery holder was cracked, but I was sure it could be fixed. It was surprisingly large because the radio required eight D batteries.

When we finally thought the radio was ready to run, we searched the house for batteries, and asked our aunts and even our classmates if they had any to spare. When we had collected more than we needed, we had to sort the good ones from the bad. We had to put them into the radio many times and check which batteries still had a charge. After many configurations, we finally combined the right batteries. Maryam turned it on and sound came from the radio! We were delirious.

My cousins and my aunt said, "You may have the radio, but do not listen all twenty-four hours. Only listen sometimes." We agreed.

We listened to many different stations on the radio. The station that caught our attention the most featured people telling stories about Jesus in strong, beautiful voices. Some were told in Pashto, others in Farsi and some in English. The program was called *Good News for All*.

We did not understand everything they said, but their voices were mesmerizing. We listened every day, and told our friends about what we'd heard. My cousins Brishna and Aruzo realized what we were listening to and said, "This is a good radio station. They broadcast good stories. But we suggest that you do not listen to this program. It will change your small brains. That will be a shame and embarrassment to our family because sometimes you tell the same stories to your classmates. And if people figure out that you are telling these stories to their kids, it will affect you and every member of this whole family. You have no idea how bad the consequences could be!"

We heard what the family said, but we did not take it very seriously. We continued to listen to the station. Sometimes the announcer asked questions about the stories, and said that listeners who mailed in the correct answers would receive books and nice notebooks. Maryam and I knew all the answers and wanted to send them, but we had two problems: postage cost twelve rupees or five cents, and we did not know how to write the answers or the address in English. Still, we were enjoying our little intrigue immensely.

By now it was summer break from school, and I was helping my uncle in his store. Our neighbor Ibrahim's shop served as both clothing store and local post office. The letter carrier's name was Aladdin. He was a very friendly man and a jokester, with green eyes and a ruddy face. The problem he had was that he could never talk quietly. He was always very loud. Also, he was very fast. He was always running with the bags full of letters. He usually stopped at Ibrahim's shop two mornings a week, delivering letters and picking up the outgoing mail.

After meeting with Aladdin more than a couple of times and drinking tea together at my uncle's shop, he became friendlier toward me. He asked me some spelling and math questions. "I heard that you are very good in school," he said. "Your uncle told me that you are very smart." Ibrahim always did the same. They both seemed to be very open-minded people, and I thought they could help me address the letter to *Good News for All*. Maryam pushed me to hurry. "You should ask them very soon," she said.

"I can ask them, but we still need twelve rupees," I replied.

"I have eggs from my chicken. I'll sell them to give you the money."

I also had a source of income. I was given a rupee sometimes for working at my uncle's shop. He always suggested that I use the money for ice cream or fruit. I gratefully accepted the money and walked around the small town. When I returned, I pretended that I had had some ice cream.

He always asked me, "What did you get today?"

I replied, "I had the best ice-cream! It was so delicious!"

In a week, we had the twelve rupees. While I was waiting for an opportune time to talk to Aladdin, I told Ibrahim that I wanted to send a letter to the BBC. I did not tell him why. Maryam and I were not sure we could trust him with our plan. Two days later, Ibrahim gave me an envelope with the address and postage already on it. It cost four more rupees, which was a lot back then, but he gave it to me for free. I ran to Maryam to tell her.

The topic of our letter was simple, "We are very interested in the radio and answers to the program called '*Your Best Answers and Gifts.*' Besides answering the radio questions, we described our life in the village. We wrote in Pashtu about the difficulties we had with the people in the village, the traditional restrictions we had to obey, and the people's beliefs about religion and culture that affected young kids like Maryam and me. We wrote about things we had seen during the war and the treatment of our family members. We shared in the letter that we did not believe in the power of the shrines and criticized the process of marrying off young girls without their permission or consent. We explained that we enjoyed their programs because they were peaceful and educational.

We worked on the letter for weeks, rewriting it five times. At the end, we wrote, "We hope you can understand our bad writing and we are so happy that we overcame our difficult problem saving so many rupees to send the letter. We cannot wait to hear about our letter on your broadcast."

I put the letter in my pocket and left it there. I kept the money that I had collected in the other pocket. Every day I waited for Aladdin, but he always came at a very busy time, when other people were around. I was becoming very distressed.

After two weeks of this, I decided to try to meet Aladdin at the bus station; that's how he took outgoing mail to the central post office. One day, right after he left my uncle's store, I told my uncle that I needed to use the bathroom outside the shop.

I ran to Aladdin while he was still at the bus station. I was lucky. He was trying to leave, but I called him, "Aladdin!"

He looked at me and asked, "What happened? Come here."

I looked around to make sure nobody can see me, then

quickly gave him the letter and money. He looked at me in disbelief. He took the money, looked at the address, and then looked back at me. I was scared, but he put his hand on my shoulder and pressed it a little. He took out two rupees, and he said, "Take these two rupees from me and buy some fruit for yourself or some candy."

I told him, "Please, the answer to this letter should not go to my uncle or Ibrahim. Please give it only to me."

"I understand that," he said. "Don't worry."

After a long day, uncle and I went home from the shop. We walked to the house, but today I was faster than my uncle because I was in a hurry to get home and tell everything to Maryam. She was talking to her mom. She saw the smile on my face and ran to me.

"Hey there! Any good news?" she inquired.

"Yes. I gave the letter to Aladdin!" I whispered.

We were very anxious to listen to the radio every single night. We did not want to miss when they talked about our letter. After almost two weeks with no word about it, we became increasingly despondent. We even wondered if Aladdin hadn't posted our letter and kept the money for himself. When he came to my uncle's shop I tried to avoid him. I thought it would be disrespectful to tell him that he was a dishonest person because he did not send our letter.

One day I admitted to him, "We have not gotten any response. This is the reason I am sad and avoiding talking to you. You took my letter and threw it somewhere in the trash."

"No, I never do that," he assured me. "You have to wait. The mail is very slow to get there. Be patient."

I told this to Maryam. She said, "Everything will be fine. Wait a little more. Aladdin is right."

Then one night, it happened. On the radio program the announcer said, "Now we turn our attention to a letter from Atal and Maryam. The letter was sent from a very long distance. We are really proud of them. They are the winners of our program. We will send gifts for them as soon as possible. They are only in the second grade. They described everything very well, and we understood each word they wrote. We also understand their difficulties." They mentioned me and that I missed my family a lot and that I hadn't seen them for two years. They also talked about the illness that Maryam had.

They continued to discuss the contents of the letter, mentioning the conflict our families had with the other people in the area because of their religion and their language. The announcers got together and prayed for us. They encouraged Maryam and me to keep in contact with them. They reassured us, "We are always with you, and God is always with you. Do not feel disappointed or heartbroken. Be strong and positive. Trust in God and always pray for yourselves. We are looking forward to hearing from you again and to having contact with you. You, Maryam and Atal, are always in our hearts, and you will be with us forever."

They discussed our letter for about five minutes. We were delirious and hugged each other.

While we were waiting for the radio station's response in the mail, we had already begun to think about writing more letters to the station and participating in their contests. But we were still worried about how to receive a letter from the radio station so that nobody would notice. The family was watching us; they were concerned that we might do something that would shame them, which could be dangerous. People might think the adults had encouraged us in our beliefs and activities.

Every time Aladdin came to pick up the mail, I looked carefully into his eyes. He just quietly signaled that there was nothing for me. I asked him several times why it was taking so long. I was worried because school was about to start, and I would not be able to meet Aladdin because he usually arrived in the morning.

Finally, one day, Aladdin walked up to me and whispered in my ear, "I have a package for you."

I was so excited, but I looked at my uncle. Hopefully, he would get busy, and I would be able to take the package. There were some people in the store, including two of my uncle's friends. While they were talking to each other, Aladdin pulled the package from his postal bag and gave it to me.

My uncle saw this and asked, "What was that?"

"These are some books from the radio station," I replied. Fortunately, he did not seem concerned.

I hid the package behind a shelf in the store, and counted the hours until quitting time. In the evening, my uncle got some groceries to take home, and he was busy closing the store. I reached my hand behind the back shelf, trembling with excitement. I took my package and slid it in a bag uncle had filled with other items. The bag was very heavy. I tried to lift it, but my uncle and my cousin Satar did not give me the chance.

"No, take the other bag," my uncle insisted. "I will take care of this heavy one."

I usually enjoyed the walk home. The fields we passed were so beautiful. My cousin and I would walk well behind my uncle so we could talk freely. We said hello to everyone we passed, even though people were still not very friendly with us. But on this walk home I walked close to my uncle, hoping to get a chance to take the package out of the bag. I babbled about this and that, just telling my uncle whatever came to mind. It did not make much sense; my goal was to distract him. My cousin was baffled by all this.

"Is everything good with you?" he asked. "You look very worried for some reason. Did my dad tell you something or do something to you?"

"No, everything is fine," I said. "He did not beat me today." He usually beat me if I sold something at the wrong price or gave something wrong to a customer.

He smiled. "Okay, you are a survivor today then!"

The time for evening prayers came, and my uncle decided to pray in a field near the house. My cousin joined him. Uncle said, "Come here and pray with us."

"I am not ready to pray," I said. "I should take *ozoo*." *Ozoo* is the method of washing one's feet, hands, mouth, and nose in preparation for prayer.

This was my chance to get the bag! I walked up to my uncle and took the heavy bag from his hands, insisting that I could carry it home. He seemed surprised but did not argue.

I got inside the house. We had four rooms around the courtyard. I set the bag in the middle room, took my package, and ran to Maryam.

Maryam's eyes lit up. "You got the package?"

"Yes."

We opened the yellow package to find several shiny

notebooks, pens, pencils, and calendars with very beautiful colors. Each page of the calendars and notebooks had writings taken from different parts of the Bible. The small notebooks described how to pray. Also, there were two small Bibles in the package. We knew that we wouldn't be able to use the calendars or notebooks because they were about Jesus and our cousins had already given us a warning.

We kept writing to the station. Each response came with more to read, more quizzes, more gifts and requests that we share the Bibles and mailing address with our family and friends. But we didn't. We kept everything hidden among the books on our bookshelf, which nobody touched.

Chapter 13

A new school semester started, so we were back at school. We were not able to study the materials from the radio program during the daytime because there were too many people around. Sometimes I carried them in my book bag when I took the animals to the hills, and pretended that Maryam and I were doing homework. Should anyone approach us, I would put the papers in the bag very quickly and bring out a schoolbook. We always got excellent scores on our returned radio quizzes.

The station kept suggesting that we tell others, and the urge to tell my very close friends, who were also my classmates, grew. I especially wanted to tell Samad and Saber, my closest friends. I always helped them with math, and they were nice to me. I asked if I could give them some notebooks and pens that I had gotten for free. They were very excited; it was very always difficult to find good school supplies. Maryam disagreed with my idea of sharing, but I felt bad that I was not doing what the radio station people had been requesting. They had promised to send us a new radio as well. We were ecstatic at the thought of a new radio and a better signal. What to do?

Finally, one day I loaded up my book bag with school supplies and headed off. I was feeling a bit hesitant knowing I had made the decision without Maryam. I prayed and said,

"Whatever comes, we will see. Samad and Saber are nice. They will not let their families know."

At the end of the school day, I gave each of the guys two pencils, two pens, three notebooks, and more. They were all beautiful colors, which pleased them a great deal. There were pens with writings and crosses on them.

"Are you really giving us these beautiful supplies?" Samad asked.

"Yes," I said. "Please keep them in your bag. When you come tomorrow, I will tell you how I got these gifts."

When I told Maryam, she wrinkled her brow and a look of disappointment crossed her face. "Hopefully," she said, "they can keep them and not show them to anyone in their families." But she didn't sound hopeful. I began to understand the gravity of the decision I'd made.

The next day, the boys came to school, opened the notebooks and began to write in them. I scolded, "Don't use those notebooks here! Keep them at home!"

Ignoring my command, Samad picked up his notebook and said, "What's going on? These writings are totally different from our subjects."

"Look," I said, "meet me at the pasture with your animals this afternoon. I will tell you the whole story then."

We we met, I told them about all of it, the radio show,

the quizzes, the letters and the packages. They understood some of what I explained about the stories. Jesus is a prophet in Islam, as are Abraham and other key figures from the Judaism and Christianity, so Muslims and Christians share many same beliefs. However, Muslim people do not believe Christ was more than a prophet, as Christians do.

A few days later I was cleaning shelves at my uncle's store when I heard a commotion in front of our shop. Three men were standing outside and shouting something. After a moment or two, I realized they wanted me to come outside the shop. Did I hear them correctly? They were going to give me a beating?

Ibrahim and my uncle stopped them and asked what was going on. One of them yelled as he waved his clenched fist, "When you got to this village with the most devout Muslims in the world, we accepted you. All of us had left our villages and our countries. We'd left behind family members, and we came here to ensure the safety of our way of life, our culture, and religion. But today we saw and heard something that we had never heard before. Nobody had said such things to our grandfathers or those before them, yet we heard something today from one in your family."

They reached into the pockets in their long vest and

pulled out several items. Watching from behind the shelves, I whispered, "God, please, help me."

The anger on their faces was unbelievable. Their bows were wrinkled, and one of the men's face and neck were very red. I could see his veins bulging as he shouted. The men held the notebooks and pens that I had given to Saber and Samad.

I was not worried for myself, but I felt so bad for my Uncle Amanullah. The men were very rude to him. He was so apologetic and pleaded with them, "Believe me, I do not know anything of this. I still do not understand. I am sorry. I apologize if they wrote something bad in those notebooks for your kids. I am sorry about that."

One of the men responded, "Your nephew did not write anything." They looked at me through the shop window. I did not budge from behind the shelves.

Amanullah asked, "If it is not about writing, could you just tell me what is wrong?" He took the notebooks from them.

"Where are you getting support from?" one of the men demanded. "Do you want to convert to a different religion?"

The third man raved, "We have kept our culture and religion for thousands of years. Nobody has the right to tell us or our families to learn a different religion. Who are you? You just came here a couple years ago, and now you started this business."

Amanullah tried to keep them calm. He asked for the contraband they'd produced from their pockets. As he handed my uncle the notebooks, the man with the reddest face spoke. "It brings shame to us that we have these notebooks and pens in our pockets. We will have to burn our clothing or beat your nephew with pencils and notebooks. We brought these notebooks as proof for you. We have brought the pens to stick in his face."

My uncle read the front of one of the notebooks, and right away, he understood. He expressed his apologies and voiced his embarrassment to everyone. I became very embarrassed, too, because I did not want my uncle and my family to be ashamed of me.

They must have believed the sincerity with which my uncle spoke. One explained to my uncle, "We will not shun you. We have not made your nephew's shamefulness known to the community. If we had told them, you would have a lot of problems for your family."

Amanullah thanked them for their kindness. He led them on their way and promised, "Do not worry, this will never happen again."

He returned to the shop, glaring at me. He searched around the shop floor to find something heavy to beat me with. He found the broom. Now was the time for me to answer for what I had done. He grabbed me and started to beat me. I was able to withstand the beating until the broom came to my head. Suddenly, I felt dizzy. The thrashing continued until my neighbor and his cousin pulled him away from me. I remember they gave me a little cold water and threw some of it on my face. I fell to the floor as I heard my uncle's scornful voice, "Get him out of my shop! I do not want to see his face."

Ibrahim took me to his shop and gave me more water. I felt a little better, but my nose was bleeding and my clothes were covered in blood. Ibrahim gave me a small blanket to cover myself. When the bleeding stopped, I started walking home. I walked to the house very fast. I did not want anybody to see me and ask me why I looked as I did. I just walked toward the house and thought about my uncle. I was feeling so guilty for the trouble I had caused him.

Everybody saw me when I reached home. They ran to me, asking, "What happened?" I got out of my bloody clothes as quickly as I could and kept quiet.

The only person I told what had really happened was Maryam because I did not want to lose my radio. "We need to take everything we have away from here," I explained.

My uncle was planning to beat me again after he came home. I did not want him to beat Maryam, too. I ran to her backpack, where she kept pencils, pens, notebooks and calendars from the radio station. I removed them, and I put them in my backpack. Next, I scurried over to the bookshelf. I removed all the books, Bibles, chapters and quizzes. I looked through all her notebooks and books carefully so as not to leave anything behind. I did not want her to be in trouble.

Elsewhere in the house, I could hear my uncles from my mom's side. They had heard about what happened and were very angry. "We are very ashamed of him," they said. "At his age, he's doing that crazy stuff? Embarrassment to the family doesn't only come from the elderly. Young people like him can do the same. I am sure he will go to hell. His face does not belong to a person who is going to heaven."

I closed and locked the door because I was scared that they might come inside, thinking that Uncle Amanullah hadn't beaten me enough. There was no place left on my body for my uncle today. For tomorrow, I was sure, he would do his business with me as well.

Later that evening, uncle returned home. He came to the room Maryam and I shared, but I had left the house. I'd run to the top of the hill closest to our house. Maryam told me that he found all the papers, which had my name on them. After checking all the rooms and gathering everything he could find, he ripped what he could to shreds and filled the kitchen stove with it. I remained on the hill until late into the night when my aunt and Maryam came and took me back home.

"You and your family treat me so bad," I complained on the way. "When my parents come, I will tell them everything."

"What are you going to tell them?"

"That my uncle beats me. I work hard for him. You see me at midnight. It is almost morning. I am out of the house, and nobody feeds me."

"Now you put everything on our shoulders. Do you really think you have not done anything wrong at all?"

"Yes," I defended myself. "That's right. I am just a boy."

"Yes," came the answer, "Everything happened because of your stupid mistakes. Are you just one kid in the whole village? Why don't the other children make any mistakes? You are the only one. Believe me, if your family hears of this, they will beat you more. You are lucky. We are giving you too much of a discount in a beating. Today, we cooked you your favorite food, red beans and yogurt with cucumbers."

When I heard about the food, I forgot everything else for the time being. I walked through the house and entered the kitchen to eat, which I did to satisfaction.

My aunt informed me, "You have no more radio, and no more books. Everything will be destroyed. Everything will be burned tomorrow." She pointed to the oven where all my books were sitting. I looked at the oven, and I became very sad. All the beautiful pens and notebooks were there. I was thinking that before she burned everything I might get something out of there. When I looked at the oven more closely I saw there were just pieces of the papers ready to be burned, so I'd not be able to salvage anything.

When I got to school the next day, my friends Saber and Samad, with whom I had been sitting for two years, were sitting in different seats in the back. The seats on my right and left were empty. The other classmates were looking at me and wondering what could have happened. I looked at my two friends and implored them to come back to their usual seats, but they refused.

The teacher entered to start the first class of the day, but rather than carrying the one usual stick for punishment in his hand, today, he had three. I had finished my homework, but was reviewing it before submitting it, so I did not look at him. I still remember the problem I was looking at — multiplying three by four — when suddenly, whack! I felt a sharp pain as the three sticks struck my shoulders. When I looked up at him, he continued to beat me. The whole class looked on in shock. The teacher had never beaten me. I was the best student in the class. Only Saber and Samad knew why.

"You are not going home after class," the teacher said. "You must stay here." He had beaten me so hard that he was exhausted. He had to pause between words to catch his breath. His wrapped head scarf, his *longee,* even started coming off his head. He beat me some more, and he would not accept my homework that day. The whole class was extremely quiet.

During the break, students went out, but I stayed at my seat gingerly touching my shoulders. They hurt a lot. And I was still in pain from the beating from my uncle the day before.

Nobody wanted to talk to me. The only person who came to me during the break was Maryam. She took from my backpack a slice of bread. She took it out and told me, "Eat." She proceeded to examine my hands and shoulders.

I looked at her. Tears were streaming from her eyes when she said, "Everything will be okay. Do you hurt very much?"

I said, "No, I am fine."

I refused to eat the bread. I was not hungry at all. My whole body was hurting. She sat with me until the end of the break. She tried to say something funny to amuse me, and I tried to make her happy, too, but I couldn't muster a smile. I still felt bad for my uncle, for how the village men had treated him when they were looking for me. And I was embarrassed by what had happened in front of my other classmates. They knew that the beating I had just endured was not the normal punishment for a student's error. The break finished and the teacher came back.

Today, we were supposed to study three subjects, but he canceled one. He said to the class, "You can go early today. I need to do some other duties. They require the remaining class time."

I was very worried. Maryam said, "I will be with you. Everything will be okay."

And so the class was dismissed. I was still sitting at my place. Maryam came closer to me. The teacher told Maryam, "You can go home."

I reiterated his instruction to her, "You should not stay here with me. Just go home." I really did not want to place Maryam in trouble. She left her seat slowly.

The teacher returned. His name was Yunus. He was not only the teacher; he was the village *mullah,* a religious leader. He led over fifty families. As *mullah,* he oversaw all the most important decisions and traditions for the village, including the resolution of most of the religious conflicts, funerals, prayers for the dead, and, of course, religious education. That was his job, and people respected him a great deal. In other words, I was now with a person who could do anything he wanted with me. He sat cross-legged in front of me on the floor.

He said, "You know, you are the best student in the class. You always do your homework. You have responsibilities in this class. You can take attendance. You write the name of the lesson at the top of the blackboard every day. You are a person that has a huge responsibility. Also, you belong to a very gracious and pleasant family. The idea to create this school was from your family. Today, you disappointed me so much. You abused the power that was given to you in this class, but let me ask you a question. There are a million people that live in this area. Look up and down all the villages. Look at the people. I have never heard of this happening anywhere else. Just tell me, how did you get the materials? Who is encouraging you? Is your family with you? Tell me the truth. I promise you that I will never tell anyone because I like you as if you were my own son."

I did not say anything, so he said, "Did you hear me? Look at me!"

I looked at him. My face and my neck were black and blue and my right eye was red. He said, "I am sorry for beating you. That was your punishment. I know it hurts, but if you give me some details, I promise you that I will not tell anyone. I am not going to suspend you from school. You can come regularly to your class. However, if you do not cooperate with me, you are done with school. I will not allow you to come here."

When I heard that, I told him, "Okay."

I started telling him about the radio programs and the letters and about the people with whom I had contact. I was completely honest about everything, except one detail.

"Is Maryam in this with you?" he asked.

"No," I said.

For one whole hour, he talked with me and gave me advice. He said, "If you do this again, something bad will happen to you. You'll be killed. It will also seriously affect your family and your uncle's family. What you did was unacceptable, and it will incite people to take violent action." Pointing to the injuries on my face and neck, he continued, "This is nothing. If you keep doing any of this — listening to the radio, sending letters and passing out such inflammatory materials — you will see what is going to happen to you. Now, you must promise that you will not bring any more *mansookh* (unnecessary item). You must not say anything to your classmates, and you yourself must not believe in this anymore. You must begin attending prayers at the mosque. This is not only to help you. You must think about your family's prestige and position here in the village, too. Other people's opinions are important for their survival, as well as yours."

"Okay," I said.

"By the way," he added, "you will not have the responsibility of taking attendance from here on in, and you will not write the topic of each lesson on the board anymore. All other responsibilities you had for the class will no longer belong to you. Now, you can go home."

I slipped out of my seat and left for home. On my way, I saw Maryam sitting next to a stone. She looked very sad and worried. "What happened?" she asked. "Did he suspend you from school? Did he beat you more?"

"No."

"Then what was the conversation about? Why did he keep you there so long?"

"He told me that I don't have any responsibilities in the class anymore. I told him about everything that we did in the past."

I went home, and my aunt had lunch for us. After that, she put olive oil on my back and neck. She massaged my neck a little. It hurt.

She told me, "Just do not do this anymore, okay?"

I answered, "Okay."

Chapter 14

After this, everything in my life changed. When I left the house to take care of the animals, my friends and my classmates would not play with me anymore. They would not even talk to me.

I tried to apologize to Saber and Samad; they had been beaten by their families for the notebooks I gave to them. Saber was willing to listen to me, and he told me, "My family said that I cannot talk to you anymore or see you either. If they catch me with you, they will beat me again very badly. Please, stay far away from me."

"I did not do anything bad," I said. "I am sure if we are nice to each other, your family will not beat you. Come on, let's play."

A couple days later, his two cousins saw that we were together. They came up to us, and one of them said, "Saber, move away from there. We told you that you cannot talk to him anymore."

Saber told his cousin, "I do not want to be friends with him anymore, but he is still pushing me."

The cousin slapped Saber's face. I just stood there. I did not want them to beat him. It was not his fault. They let him go, but they picked up some stones from the ground. They were very sharp. They started beating me on my head and face. I tried to defend myself as best I could, but I did not want to fight with them. I repeated over and over, "What did I do wrong?"

They cut me in several places on my head and forehead with those sharp stones. They beat me until I stopped talking and was unable to move, then one of the cousins said, "It's enough." I wiped my nose and mouth, which were full of blood. They ran off and left me lying in the dirt on the side of a hill, far away from the house. Maybe I passed out for some time; I am not sure. I heard my name being called, and noticed that the sky was getting dark. I had great difficulty just getting to my feet. I did not have enough energy to answer the calls, but lucky for me, they knew where to look for me because I was not far from my usual spot where I studied and looked after the animals. When my aunt and Maryam found me, my head was on the ground, and my face was covered in blood. As they helped me to my feet, Aunt Aisha asked me, "Who beat you? We should break their hands. God will punish them."

Maryam and my aunt helped me to get to the house. We had to go very slowly. I remember I was so thirsty. Maryam and my aunt Aisha were crying. I was trying to be brave and tried to smile for them. I said, "Do not say that we will break their hands. Let's ask God to give them peace."

At home, they washed my head and my face and put

some bandages on my head. I told them not to tell my uncle what really happened. "Just tell him that I was climbing up one of giant stones in the pasture, and I fell down and hit my head," I said. I did not want to create any problems between Saber's cousins' family and my uncle's family. That family had a lot of power and influence, and we were already facing enough difficulties.

I wanted to forget what had happened, and I hoped that people would forget what I had done, and that they would forgive my family and me. I was very lonely at this time. Even with Maryam on my side, I felt as if I were alone in the world with no support from anyone. The family told me again and again, "You are not going to do anything like this anymore. If you do it in the future, we will send you away from the house. Where will you go? Your family will not be proud of you and what you were doing. Do you want to become a doctor? Pay attention to your school subjects!"

For many months I did not go into the town. I stayed at home or took the animals to the hill. One lucky day, something urgent came to my teacher. He cancelled classes for the whole grade for an entire week. At this same time, my relationship with my uncle was showing a little bit of improvement. He asked me if I could help him in the store for a week. I was so excited because I was going back to the town. I ran to the shop, and I saw my friends and the shopkeepers from the neighboring shops. I said hello to each of them. I started organizing the shelves, cleaning floors, and sorting products.

When Aladdin arrived I greeted him, but when he saw me, he stopped for moment. He came closer to me as he looked around. My uncle was not in the shop. He leaned down to me and said, "Your packages are still coming. Your uncle warned me not to give anything to you. Because of you, my job is in danger."

He quickly took the packets out from his bag and showed them to me. There were five. He said, "I cannot throw your packages in the garbage because it is against the post office policy. This is my job! You must write to the radio station and tell them not to send anything to this address again. I cannot help you anymore. You must write the letter. The day after tomorrow I am going to come here again, and I will pick it up."

"Yes," I said, nodding in agreement.

I hid the packages at the back of the shelves that were not used much. I decided I would take one each day and give it to Maryam. My relatives were always checking my book bag, but no one checked hers. Maryam took all the letters, too, and she burned all of them. I was lucky. No one saw us.

To please Aladdin, I wrote a letter and explained the situation. I asked that they stop sending me letters and packages for now. I expressed my concerns about my uncles' families and other relatives, and promised them that I would contact them in the future. When Aladdin arrived, I slipped him the envelope. I also offered him twelve rupees that Maryam had given me, but he said he would pay the postage.

Around this time, we learned that the story that I gave the notebooks to Saber and Samad had spread from family to family. The women and girls in my uncle's family usually went all the way to the well to get water in the evenings. The women had to cross through the whole village. One day, they were going to get the water. Some teenagers from the village taunted them by shouting, "Hey, *kafir* infidel!"

The teenagers kept doing this for many weeks. When my aunt could take it no longer, she told one of my male cousins not to let the teenagers and their families say these disrespectful words anymore.

My cousin Satar was not a patient person, and he confronted the teenagers. They argued, and he slapped some of them in their faces.

A few weeks later, I was tending the animals and working on my homework. I was drawing a flower when I looked up and saw that five people were coming toward me.

Some of them had sticks, and some of them had stones in their hands. I stood up, thinking, "I did not do anything wrong."

They came up to me and said, "You think it is so easy for your family members to slap somebody in the face?"

I offered my apologies to them; at this time, I did not know what had happened between my cousin Satar and the teenagers. They didn't listen, just started beating me in the head with the sticks and stones. I got dizzy. Someone saw what was happening and told my aunt. When she and Maryam found me, my books were torn up, my board for math was broken and I was using the flower drawing to wipe some of the blood from my face.

As they led me home, I said, "I did not do anything bad."

They brought me home and put new bandages on me again. This was becoming a usual activity. The villager kids were starting to tease me about it, saying, "If you stay here, you will never remove your bandages."

My many wounds healed little by little. I kept going to school. Maryam was a huge support for me. Time moved fast and my life changed. I learned how to write. By the time I reached eleven, I had finished with the village school and started attending the town school, twenty kilometers away. Girls were not welcome.

Word came that my parents were going to come to our area soon. I was excited. My life would change. I was counting the weeks.

Chapter 15

Finally, in 1998, they arrived in my village. My parents and my sister, Seema, joined us. A long time had passed since I had seen them. My dominant language had changed. My attire changed, too. I was constantly wearing a prayer cap. We looked at each other, and we no longer looked like we were from the same family. Still, it was a grand reunion. I was excited and happy, and we hugged each other. They had missed me a lot. I was their only son.

Everybody asked about the scars of my face. I did not want to make them sad, so I did not tell them about the beatings. "If you live in the village with animals and jungles," I said, "then it is required to have scars on your face."

My sister told me, "You have completely changed. You learned Pashto very fast. You have forgotten Dari. How is school?"

"School is good. But there are no schools here for girls."

They said, "We know. We hope we can go to a better place some day."

Many uncles and cousins got together with us. We had fun and happiness. I had missed my mom's hugs, yet, I guess, because of the length of our separation, I wasn't comfortable with her arms around me. I was already grown up enough, so she should not keep me in her embraces anymore, but still, to her I was her baby boy.

When my family settled, they shared stories about the war in Kabul and their neighbors' deaths. Our neighborhood had been destroyed, including our home, which had previously been looted a number of times. Now that they had come here, it was time to start over, build a new house and create a new life from ground up. In one sense, it sounded simple, but I knew that my family would have some trouble living here among these villagers.

I moved from Maryam's house to my family's temporary home, which was really Uncle Manan's room for his livestock. Still, we were together at last. Soon, we built two more rooms for our family. They were made by mixing stones with clay and water for walls. All my uncles and cousins helped. I started my new life with my family.

Life went on, but not without its challenges. First, my Uncle Amanullah still had his shop, but because the income was not enough to support his family, he was trying to obtain a visa to go to work to a different country. My sister was trying to fit into her new environment. She tried to dress in the clothes that other villagers were wearing. The clothes were not exactly from the village, but still were more appropriate than her typical city clothes. Now she had to deal with villagers like Aruzo and Brishna did.

Much to my surprise, my father was stricter than my Uncle Amanullah. He looked at my books from school. Most of them were so-called religious, and were about war with non-Muslim people. He was not happy about the contents. But I was surprised to learn that he was more religious than my uncles. He believed in Islam more than my uncles appeared to. However, the villagers did not believe he was sincere. They felt he was only putting on an act to be accepted by them. My father had a lot of disagreements with the village people. He did not agree with what they believed.

The villagers were no more accepting of my mother and sister, but they did like to complain to them about me. The women told them everything about me. They told them, too, that it was bad that they immigrated from Afghanistan so late and converted to a different religion. My family was very angry at me for the trouble I'd caused them. My father and my mom warned, "You should not have done that. You embarrassed us. We understand now why you have so many scars on your face. You must never do those things again."

Nonetheless, I was looking for the opportunity to get into contact with that radio station again. I was weighing the pros and cons very carefully and considering my options. I did not want to create any problems again, but I wondered what the people at the radio show thought about me. Not being able to listen to the radio anymore, I was not sure if the radio station still existed. But I considered them friends, and it is not in my personality to forget friends, even though I could create trouble for myself. It had been three long years since I had had any contact with the radio group, and by now I was in seventh grade in school. The pain of the beatings was fading, so I was not as afraid as I should have been.

One day, I decided to send a letter with a different return address. I sent them the address of one of my mom's cousins, the first place I had stayed when I arrived in Pakistan some years before. It was the only place I could think of since I had no friends to trust at school. This new address was twenty kilometers farther from my house to the west in a village called Tal. The family in Tal had a grocery shop. Our two families kept in close contact with each other. I chose their address without asking them.

I wrote, "This is Atal. I have been stuck in my troubles, and my family from Kabul came here. I hope you still remember my name and my letters to you." I sent the letter, and I waited for a response. However, I had no idea when the package would arrive at the shop in Tal. I couldn't go there after school because I was expected at Uncle Amanullah's shop to help him and my father. I decided that my only choice was to skip school every Thursday to go and check if the package had arrived.

I went one Thursday, but there was no package. I told Bakht Yar, the owner of the shop, that I should be getting a package. I didn't explain anything else. Bakht Yar said he would do this, but I was somewhat apprehensive. I did not want my mail to remain in their shop for a long period of time.

I returned to my uncle's shop that day. Nobody caught on that I had skipped my classes. I focused finding some money for transportation. From then on I did not spend a single rupee that my family would give me to buy lunch at school.

On the third Thursday, there was a package for me. It was already opened. Bakht Yar was very angry. He yelled at me, "I absolutely will not accept your packages at this shop! You are not to do this anymore. I know all about what you did four years ago. Have you started again?" He shoved the package at me and threw me out of his shop.

I walked away sad and disappointed that Bakht Yar had treated me so. I took the letter from the already opened envelope to read as I walked. The letter said that the people from "Good News for All" were very excited and happy about me contacting them again after all this time. They wrote, "We have been thinking about you and worrying about you. Now we are glad to learn that you are still in God's peace. We are happy to have read your beautiful writing with words of loyalty to us. We are also happy to hear that you did not forget about us. God helps you! We will always be with you." They included some verses from the Bible about peace and loyalty and being with God. I was elated to read the encouragement from them. I folded the letter and put it back in the envelope. Inside were pamphlets with Bible stories about people who also had difficulties in their lives.

My happiness faded again as I realized I did not have another option for receiving letters from them. Then I thought of something. The letter included a telephone number. "You can always call us," it read. "If it is possible, we can advise you and help you. Make sure when you call us, that you are in a safe place. Do not share the number with anyone. Go to a place where people cannot figure out who you are calling or overhear your conversation."

Off I went to find a PCO (Public Call Office). When I got to one, and showed the clerk my two rupees, he said I would be able to talk for two minutes. I had never used a phone in my life. I thought, "How expensive!"

I told the PCO agent the number I was calling. I told him, "I will need a private place for the call." He showed me the special booths. He also showed me how to hold the phone. I had never even touched a telephone in my life!

I dialed the number. I was breathing very hard and fast. My hands were shaking. The phone rang.

The person on the other end of the phone said, "Hello, this is Shams."

I started to talk to him and introduced myself very fast.

He said, "We are very happy to hear from you! God bless you that you are still alive at your age and in this time of conflict. We understand the situation you are in. It is very dangerous in that area. Please try to stay safe."

"Thank you, but I have only two minutes to talk, and, please, I have no place where I can receive or keep my packages because my family doesn't allow me to have them. They warned me that I mustn't get any more packages from you."

"Please contact the post office and tell them to hold your packages. Your city's post office workers are very nice people. We believe they will help you." He made it very short, but I got the idea. Shams wanted to say something else, but the two minutes ended. Our time was up. His idea was very helpful. I left the PCO office, and I asked people on the street where the main post office was.

The post office was in a building that had a lot of other

governmental offices. Police officers stood at the front door. They checked my clothes, and they found the package that I had in my hands. The officer said, "We should check what this is." He took the package from my hand and looked inside. "How shameful this is!" he said. "You should be ashamed of yourself. Do you have any family? How are you still alive here?" He threatened me with a gun.

I realized that he was doing this just for the amusement of the other officers. He pushed the end of the gun into my stomach; I tried to get my package and letter back from him. More policemen came and surrounded me. One of the workers crossed the area, and he asked, "What's happening?"

The policeman answered, "Nothing. He is trying to go inside."

The worker said, "You must let him go immediately. Is there any reason you are holding him?"

The policeman said to me, "You can go inside."

The letter was still in his hand. I told the worker, "He's got my letter, and he doesn't want to give it back to me."

The worker, a manager or supervisor there, walked to the officer, so the officer gave the letter to me at that very moment. The policemen glared at me and said, "Stupid refugee." He wore a long beard and held religious beads in the hand not holding the gun.

The worker who had helped me said, "Let me know whatever you need, and I will help you. I am the manager here." He had a very nice smile. "Don't worry," he said. "My son is your age. Your family must be proud of you. You are going to the post office by yourself. My son is not smart enough to go somewhere by himself yet. By the way, my name is Kausar." He gave me a hand, and we went inside.

I responded, "I am Atal."

He asked, "For what reason are you here today? Do you want to send a package to somebody? You look worried. Do not worry. The police officers are rude. I know that they bother the refugees around here. Anyway, I am here always to help you. You look exactly like my son." He gave me a hug. He said, "Give me your package. I will send it for you."

"Mr. Kausar, I am not sending any packages today. If I show you something, promise that you will not be mad at me."

He looked at me in surprise and responded, "I will never be angry. This is my job. If something is related to my job, it will be my pleasure to help you. If you are here for some other reason, I deeply apologize, but I will not be able to help you. Tell me first what reason brought you here today."

"I have been in contact with this radio station," I said, then told him the whole story. "A couple of hours ago, I called those people from the radio station who sent me letters and school supplies, and they suggested that somebody from the post office could help me and I could receive packages here. If you are still not mad at what I said, please help me."

He seemed very surprised. He put his hand on my head and said, "I cannot believe that you can speak in this way. That was a very nice story. Look at me. I am a very open-minded person. What you believe and what you want to learn really makes me proud of you. I can help you with that. It is my job. You must be careful in the future with the community you live in and with your family. There are many dangers in what you are doing. You may not know that. So be very careful! That is my advice to you. Your packages will always be safe with me, but I cannot guarantee that your life will be safe. You should not tell anyone my name because my job will be at risk. You are a child. You cannot decide what is good and what is bad. Nonetheless, you are a very brave person. I wish I had known everything as you do when I was your age. Don't worry. You can stop here once a week."

I was so grateful and happy. I had a huge smile on my face. I fully trusted him after hearing his words.

He asked, "Is there anything else I can help you with today?"

I said, "No."

"Off you go now. Be safe! If they still bother you when

you come to the door next time," he said, pointing to the police, "tell them my name, and I will be there for you. They will never stop you again."

I walked through the main door to leave. The policemen were still staring at me. "Somebody will get you," said one. But I was too happy to let his remark bother me. I left the building still smiling and ran to the bus.

"How was school today?" my father asked when I arrived at my uncle's shop, right on time.

"Everything was fine," I said. I had already hidden the package where nobody could find it.

Chapter 16

Over the next year, I maintained regular communication with the radio station, skipping school on Thursdays and getting punished for it. Mr. Kausar occasionally offered me cookies or tea. I learned that he was originally from Panjab, the area where most Christian people in Pakistan live.

At the end of the school year, attendance was very important. One of my classmates remarked, "You are lucky you have two days off. You have Thursday and Friday off."

I replied, "Thursday is not my day off. I have many matters to attend to on Thursdays."

"What is it that you do?" he asked again and again.

I only told him, "I will tell you some day, not now."

In spite of the missed days, I never did poorly in school. I still had excellent grades, especially in math and science. I was very interested in these two subjects. I even kept my grades up in religious studies, though the teacher had never liked me. My questions often made him angry. Most were questions about situations I had seen as a little boy, when women were treated badly. I asked him why women had no say in choosing whom they would marry. I wanted to know why the girls couldn't go to school the same as the boys. I asked why they couldn't walk alone. I wasn't trying to make trouble, I was trying to understand what I had witnessed with Latifa, Zarina and Maryam. They were always on my mind, and I felt weak and guilty for not helping them. That's what fueled my questions.

One morning before class started, several of us were discussing math problems when the principal and the religion teacher entered the classroom. Both carried big wooden switches. I knew whatever was about to happen couldn't be good. The principal walked down the row to where I was sitting on the floor and told the students gathered around me to move out of the way. The principal was a middle-aged man, tall and thin, and although he was often angry, he generally was friendly to me.

The teacher shouted, "Stand up immediately! Now!" He seized my backpack (which was really only an old blue chador that I wrapped around my books and supplies each day) and emptied it out.

Then they checked my *wascut* (coat), and they started checking the pockets of my *qamees* (long Shart) and pants. I knew that next he would check the front pocket of my Shart, which held a special notebook with a Christian calendar and Bible verses. I covered the pocket with my hand. The teacher put two heavy sticks into one hand, raised his arm and brought it down against my hand. My hand went numb immediately, but I kept it in place.

The principal and teacher hit my hand again and again. The teacher may have thought this was his chance to beat all the questions from my mind. They hit me until they broke all the switches they had brought and my hands were bloody and bruised. Then they took the calendar, which had the contact information written inside.

"We will show you how to enjoy every Thursday off," the principal said, then led me to his office and closed the door. He showed me the attendance record and all the Thursdays I had missed.

"We sent a letter to your father," he said. "We gave him a thorough account, including the positive accomplishments you have been making in school and your good grades. We told him that you are a very polite boy. We told him that we really love you, and you have a special space in every teacher's heart in this school. In the response we got, your father told us that there was no excuse for you to have been missing school on Thursdays. Your uncle gave us the full right to do whatever we need to do to get information from you. They want to know what you are doing when you are not in school. You must be honest with me. If you are honest, I will not beat you anymore and I will not suspend you from school."

So then I explained about my Thursday trips to the post office. I had promised Kausar that I would not tell anyone his name, and so I didn't. I had also promised my sister who had been helping me hide my packets that I would never tell anyone she helped, and I kept that promise, too.

"Do you meet with anyone around the area that gives you information about these people?" asked the principal.

"No," I answered.

"Do they give you a salary for this?"

"No, there is no one," I repeated.

"Do you practice praying?"

"Yes, I pray every day, five times."

He kept probing for details, so I explained everything, the radio station, the letters to the program and the packages. I told him about the difficulties at the post office. I asked him to promise not to tell my family that I had been keeping in contact with the radio station all this time, and he said he wouldn't tell them, but he did not keep his promise.

By this time school had let out, so he let me go, too. When I got to the shop, my uncle and my father were waiting for me. My uncle began by telling me that they had received a letter from my principal. My father looked at the condition of my hands and remarked, "It seems that they beat you badly."

They kept me in the shop the whole afternoon. I realized that uncle and father did not want to let the people in the village know what had happened, and they would try to keep it secret. I was sure they were going to punish me when I got home. I just did not know how it would happen. I worried also about what might happen to my sister and Maryam.

In the evening, we walked to the house. Nobody wanted to talk to me while we were walking. They looked at me like I had committed a huge crime. My older cousin, who was usually very friendly with me, looked extremely angry that evening. He did not even want to walk on the same path with me on the way home. The house was quiet when we arrived. My mother saw the blood on my hands and asked, "What happened?"

"Nothing," I said. "My teacher beat me a little bit."

I wanted to find a moment alone with Maryam to warn her and let her know that something was going on with my uncle and father. I wanted to tell her that they found out why I missed a lot of days at school. My parents were sitting with me, so I couldn't get to her. My uncle told me that I was not allowed to leave the house that night.

At dinner time we went inside and I sat in the corner. My heart was jumping and my hands were shaking. My uncle Amanullah and cousin Satar and Manan, my maternal uncle, and his two sons Rahim and Hejrat were in the room also. Uncle Amanullah said, "We got another letter from your school, and it came this afternoon. It says that you missed classes. They wrote that you were going to the post office in Tal. Can you tell us the reason why you have been going there for the whole year?"

I had no answer for them. I just sat there quietly in the corner, but they kept pushing me. Finally, I told them the truth. I added, "I think it is not a crime or anything bad. I decided to learn something different and have contact with other people. The people around the area in our village believe in something that is very unacceptable to me."

"You are very young, and you should not think this way," countered Uncle Manan. He was very religious. "Many foreigners have come and brought their ideas, but we never accepted them. We have kept our culture for thousands of years. You were told several years ago not to get any letters from them. We told you we don't want the children here to learn about these things. You already knew the consequences and that people would persecute both you and the whole family. You were punished every single day, and yet you decided to defy us and repeat the same thing again and again? Tell me where the pamphlets and letters are."

"They belong to me," I said. "I cannot allow anyone to

232

check my personal belongings."

My cousin Satar slapped me in the face. Satar had become a very strict and religious person and cared a lot about the family's reputation. Then my mother, who had heard my defiant words from the other room, rushed in and slapped me as well. My cousin began to beat me, but my uncle said, "Let him finish what he has to say."

I was so disillusioned. It was the first time my mom had ever hit me. I hadn't expected Satar to slap me either. I wiped tears from my eyes and blood from my lip. I did not care about the pain; my tears were for my disappointment in these two people.

Still they kept asking about the papers. They warned me, "If you do not show us, we will find your boxes and the papers. It is better to beat you, so you give us everything." I remained silent because I knew the packages were with my sister Seema and Maryam. Uncle Manan and Satar started beating me.

My poor mother was so miserable. She was torn because I was her son and it was unacceptable for someone to beat me in front of her. She left the room, then quickly returned with all of the missing pamphlets and papers. My father was shocked. He mistakenly thought she had been keeping them that he began to rant at her. Hearing this, Seema ran in and announced, "I kept the packages!" My father smacked her face. Satar, who was stronger than everybody in the room, hit her on the back with a metal poker from the tandoor, hurting her badly. I attempted to protect her, but I was not able to fight him off. They beat us both.

"There are no more chances for you!" Uncle Manan declared. "You can choose to change your mind, or your family will be in trouble. You know that you will be killed very soon if you keep doing this."

I said I wouldn't.

Everything, all the pamphlets, letters, packages were burned immediately. Then they beat Maryam that night, although they were not even sure about her involvement, they only suspected. They did not want to beat her too much because they knew she was going to marry soon.

After that night, the house was quiet for a very long time. The family checked my room, bags, and boxes every day. I felt so lonely. I felt bad for Seema because of her injury. She was taking medication for the pain. Maryam was still with me, but the days for her to get married were coming closer and closer.

My relationships with other villagers changed a lot, too. People became even more disrespectful to my family and me, harassing us for all kinds of reasons. At school, the news of my being found out spread quickly among our classmates. I think it was Saber who started the rumors. I heard that the religion teacher also told students about the calendar and religious things I'd been hiding. He even called me the devil in one lesson. As a result, students often taunted me with questions about my "devilish beliefs." No one wanted anything to do with me.

Still, my beliefs did not change. I often argued with my uncles. I maintained that people in the area were not following their religion, Islam, but were following the Pashtonwali, "laws" which were not part of the religion. That was my way of showing my defiance toward what people in that area believed in, especially the Pashtun. Our arguments and my reasons spread to my classmates' houses.

The area was getting more intolerant, and people became more religious and focused on traditions and culture because the biggest school for Taliban fighters was in Kahi, my village. Restrictions about many activities increased; for example, people could no longer listen to music or play music, and of course there was no singing. Everyone, men and women, had to wear head coverings. The women and girls wore chadors while the men and boys wore turbans and prayer caps.

This was a dangerous time. But I never stopped thinking

about the people at the radio station.

Chapter 17

The end of the school year was approaching, and a huge celebration was being planned. Students were divided into groups, and each group had responsibilities. Lots of student presentations and performances were also planned. I decided to participate. I wanted to make a small presentation, so I asked the principal if I could. Immediately he stated that he would need to check my presentation.

During class on the day students were practicing their presentations, the language teacher listened, checked for their appropriateness, and gave students suggestions. My presentation was about the difficulties my family had had in the village and all the ideas that I had gotten from the radio station. I showed the outline to my teacher. He tore the paper into pieces, saying, "Do it again." The next day, I rewrote my presentation on the same topic but with different words. This time when my teacher read it, he tore it up and gave me two slaps across the face. "You must change the content," he said.

I went home and asked Aruzo to help me. With her help, I managed to prepare my presentation in time for the end-of-school party. This time the teacher approved my outline, not knowing that it was incomplete.

The end of the semester celebration arrived, and our

presentations began. I patiently waited my turn, reviewing my planned speech in my head. I walked on the stage, made by the students from mud, stone, planks of wood, and a big woven red rug.

I started my presentation with the experiences that I'd had when I got to the area. That part was interesting to the audience. Then I got to the part where teachers beat me. Next, I explained my disagreement with their cultural beliefs. Why were beatings acceptable here? I said that I did not think it was dangerous to hear about another religion. Maybe there was something to be learned from all religions. Next, I told them that it made me so angry to return from school each day and see my female relatives sitting at home, unable to go to school. It was good to allow all children, boys and girls, to study.

With each utterance I became more passionate. Near the end of the presentation, I was in a very highly emotional state, and I started to speak loudly, so everybody could hear me. I did not feel any fear.

"Can you tell me why girls can't go to school? Can you tell me why I had to be ostracized because my first language was not yours? Can you tell me how it is you think you can judge someone's sincerity to a religion? Is it written on our foreheads?"

The auditorium was silent. Students stared at me in

shock. The teachers looked at each other in disbelief. I continued to talk as two students who were assigned to provide security for the celebration came to the front of the stage. The teachers told them, "Kick him off the stage."

I was saying that these Pashtuns had to let people learn about other cultures and religions and bring peace to their community, but the security guards did not let me complete my presentation. A group of older students gathered in front of the stage. They wanted to attack me, but they were prevented by the teachers.

The "security" held me by my shoulders and hit me. I continued with my speech until they pushed me outside.

My mother had prepared rice, meat, beans, and potatoes for the party, so I headed to the ninth-grade tent. I thought perhaps I could join the party, but I was not allowed. As the other students from the village went home happily from the party with their report cards, I went home empty-handed and disappointed that my speech had not swayed anyone.

Everybody at home asked how my presentation went. I told them, "The presentation was good, but they did not let me finish." When I was asked why, I told them I didn't understand why because I hadn't said anything bad. I had asked some questions because we were going to school to learn, I said, but no one had answers.

I was worried about my father's questions about my grades because I did not have any to show him. As I waited for him to come home, I wondered what punishment he would give me. I was tired of the beatings and restrictions, which were getting worse and worse.

In the evening, my father returned from the shop. I tried not to join the family for dinner, but my father called me into the room where they were eating. He pulled my report card from his pocket.

"I know why you did not come to eat dinner with us," he said. "We have your grades, thanks to one of your teachers who came to our shop today. He gave me your grades and a letter. The letter states you were excellent in school this term. It also mentioned your presentation today. Apparently, you added some extra parts to it that your teacher had never seen, even though they told you not to talk about it. Then the teacher accused you of getting a salary or some other support from a non-Muslim agency to spread evil ideas. Last, the teacher said that you are expelled from school." He put the expulsion form in my hand. "You cannot return."

One of my uncles shouted that because of me, they almost came to blows with the teacher. Out of respect for the teacher, they did not hit him, but the scene was very ugly.

The whole family was so very disappointed in me and unhappy. They did not want to listen to me explain anything. I had lost their trust.

My father lamented, "We do not know what to do with you."

Uncle Amanullah and Satar offered me three choices. The first choice was to be a mechanic. The second choice was to be a shopkeeper. The third choice was to be a shepherd.

I said, "I am going back to school."

"You have a couple of days to think about this," Amanullah said to me. "We are very tired of you. You've caused too many problems. Why did you not die somewhere?"

"You have made our lives miserable," Satar added in an agonized way.

I ran to my aunts, mom, and sister for support. "Look at my grades!" I said. "I am first in the class. Please tell them not to take me out of school. I can do the hardest job for them, but please, let me stay in school."

My mother was willing to listen to me. Even though I was already expelled, she seemed to agree with my choice. She said, "Maybe Atal will be the only person in our family to become a doctor or an engineer."

One of my aunts said, "Yes, he makes mistakes.

Certainly, he is different from our family in some ways, but he has seen a lot of difficulties and death."

Another added, "The teachers and students have beaten him. As a result, he could have a mental problem. Let him try for a normal life. He is learning a lot day by day."

The women appealed to the men. The men listened to them, and I was lucky; they again gave me a last chance.

My cousins Satar, Aziz and Hejrat, however, warned me that they would kill me soon, and they were very serious about it. They were studying religion in *madras* (religious school), and with each lesson, they became more militantly religious. This manifested as control over the girls and women in the house just as they were already required to do if they left their property. They ordered all of our female family members to cover themselves in the house and outside, always to pray, and not to laugh or smile. I completely disagreed with what they were doing. They did not want girls to study much. They believed that women should study how to pray and that was all.

I took my suspension paper and went back to school three weeks later. I headed to the principal's office, but he did not allow me to enter the school grounds. I did not feel any fear, but my heart was beating so hard. I offered my apology, but he did not accept it. "You are not a student here," he said.

"We cannot help you. I am so embarrassed to have had such a student, and I would be embarrassed to allow such a student as you to return. With these evil ideas that you are getting from your family, we do not want you back."

Soon after that, my father went to the mosque to pray and was told that he was not welcome there anymore. None of my family was welcome to any events, not celebrations, not even funerals. Even the small kids in the village no longer said hello to anyone in our family.

In the next few days, I went to different schools, but their monthly fees and tuition were very high. Finally, I found a school that would accept me, but it was fifty kilometers from my house. I was asked why I'd left my previous school. I was afraid to admit the truth, so I said simply, "I am interested in studying here." My grades were good, so that was enough. I woke up very early in the morning to catch the bus that took me there.

By this time, I had reached tenth grade. I worked hard and tried not to make mistakes. I did not bring up anyone's beliefs. I had a religion teacher that always talked about how good Sunni were and how bad Shia were. The students believed him and they often talked about the *kafir* Shia. This disturbed me, but I managed to hold my tongue.

In the back of my mind, I was still always trying to figure out how to contact the radio station. The people there understood my difficulties. I was driven to know why people reacted so negatively to me, why people beat me, why it was so dangerous for the whole family. I did not understand. Everything from the Christian perspective seemed better, especially for women, who were treated with respect. The people from the radio station wanted equal education for all. It impressed me profoundly, and I wanted to learn more about their beliefs. On the other hand, I felt so bad for my family. The disappointment was there. They disagreed with my ideas as much as I disagreed with theirs.

Besides learning about Christianity and its tenets, my goal was to have close contact with the people from the radio station and participate more. I hoped that one day I could speak to people and tell everyone that Christianity is not as bad as people thought. I had not seen any words in the pamphlets that should have caused such a negative reaction. In contrast, Islam kept the women hidden and denied them freedom. That was an overpowering thought, and it was important for me to teach people to interpret their religion in the right way, to translate their book, the Koran. The Pashtun did not know what the Koran was about. They believed it was good to read thirty chapters of the Koran. In fact, they held celebrations when the thirty were read. But they did not understand a word of it because it was in Arabic. I did not believe that reading something without any meaning made sense. My family and friends disagreed with me. They explained that everything in the Koran came to Mohammed in Arabic, and that God said to learn your religion in the Arabic language. But women and girls had no idea what Islam or the Koran were. They only kept a Koran at home and kept it covered with cloths of five different colors to show their respect. And sometimes when they had difficulty, they took out the Koran and kissed it. But they knew little of what was inside.

Sometimes when a person traveled or headed out for an important function, their family and friends would waive the Koran over their heads. These were the same people that beat their family members and told them to read the Koran, but they did not know what they were reading. I did not like that men were allowed to have up to five wives at the same time, too.

I often asked my mother, "Mom, do you read the Koran? Do you understand what you are reading?"

She usually got angry at me and did not continue this conversation. She said, "Reading the Koran is more important than your studying. Forget about understanding; Koran is our lives."

But one day, in front of everyone, I refused to drop it.

"There is more to understand there," I insisted. "Look at our family; I am the only person that is in school. My cousins go to the *madras*. Nobody has the opportunity to go to school for a better life. I saw how they promised Maryam to someone who she would never meet until the marriage takes place. What about Zahir? Zahir married a fifteen-year-old girl without her agreement when he was fifty-five. And mom, what about Latifa and her sickness? She died in an animal pen. Does the Koran say to act like this? Is it taught in this book of yours to treat people poorly and to kill people like Uncle Shar Khan? He did not commit any crime. He was just the head of the household. His murderers are still alive. What will happen to his two daughters? What is the solution that this book gives? Is this the way to heaven?"

I spoke very emotionally without fear of anything. "Nobody from this community, from this area, nobody will go to heaven," I declared.

My aunts looked surprised. One sarcastically remarked, "Your body needs some more massage." Of course, I understood that "massage" meant beating. Another aunt gave me a stern look and said, "The families here believe this, and they could shoot you very easily, and we will not protect you."

"I am not afraid of these people," I said. "I wish I could get to that radio station and say all these same things not only to you but also on the radio, so everybody could hear this. Who will judge me? Who's going to kill me? God or a person? I am very honest. These thoughts are always on my mind. Nobody can change my ideas, even if you beat me or shoot me with a bullet in my forehead. These are my beliefs, and I will die for them. I only want to educate people to improve the treatment of women and to accept education for women."

No one's beliefs changed, but I persisted. I explained what I learned from the pamphlets I was sent. At least it was translated into Pashto, I added, so that I could understand what I was reading. I reminded them of the respect for women and belief in education for all.

I pointed out the issues we dealt with where we lived. If somebody got very sick and needed serious medical treatment, the family had to go to the whole community, knock on doors to raise the money to visit a country that was not Muslim — and the person usually survived. Were the non-Muslims we went to for help, some of whom were women, different humans? Did those women doctors not have any father, brothers or uncles? Were they more capable than our women? Did God really insist that only men could be doctors, and women cleaners?

No one in my family would answer. The only thing they

always said was it was a big sin to talk about religion in this way.

Only Maryam and my sister Seema, who still suffered backaches from the beating, agreed with me, quietly. So when I resolved to contact the radio station again, they gave me money for the call.

I visited the Public Call Office in Hangu. There were only two telephones there, and many people hanging around, waiting for calls. I decided to leave and try again when it was less crowded so there would be less risk of being overheard. But it was crowded every time I went, so I tried anyway, hoping no one would listen.

When I got through, I talked with Taher. He remembered me immediately. "We are so glad that you are still with us!" he said. "You are the only person from that area who contacts us. We believe in your interest and that you are a very open-minded person. God gave you a good feeling for other people, especially for women. We are always praying for you. We are so glad and pleased that you can still deal with your difficulties. We know the area. We highly encourage you to bring some more people here. We are hoping that God's peace will come to them, too, and people will understand our goals. Be strong and keep calling us every week. Our pastor is very interested in talking with you."

I wanted to tell Taher that I had Maryam and Seema to support me, but in my culture it was very rude to talk about women in a conversation with men, so I didn't mention them. Ten minutes and almost forty rupees later, the phone call ended.

When I paid the operator, he asked me, "That was a very long conversation. Which company supports you?"

"No company! I was just talking with friends."

He looked at me very suspiciously. Forty rupees was a lot to spend on a phone call. But because of Taher's encouragement, I was happy. He was the first person who told me that what I was doing was right. I felt special, and I believed that I might work at the radio station someday. I wanted to discuss women and encourage people to work towards peace.

Later, I reported everything to Maryam and Seema, "I talked with Taher. He is the only person besides you that encourages me. He said I am the only one from this area to contact the station. When I meet with everyone there face to face, I will tell them that I have some family support. I really wanted to tell them that I am not the only person and that there are three of us. Do not be upset at me for not mentioning you. When I meet them, I will tell them everything."

"You do not have to tell them," Seema said, smiling. "God can see us. We did not do anything bad."

I told them that the pastor wanted to talk to me, but I was out of money. They promised to help me earn more.

In the meantime, we talked about what to tell the radio people and tried to anticipate what they might ask me. Seema said she believed that they wanted to start a Christian community in our area. I thought that was probably impossible, but I still dreamed of sharing my beliefs on the air.

Raising money was difficult. When we had twelve rupees I decided to call again, hoping that three minutes would be enough. Maryam and Seema warned me to be careful not to let anyone else hear what I was saying.

The PCO was crowded, as usual. When it was my turn, I gave the number to the same operator. He had a big beard, red eyes and uncomfortable-looking clothes, and held prayer beads in his hands. A gun was hanging on his right shoulder, and he was surrounded by religious pictures he'd hung around the room. He looked at the number, then at me. "You are calling the same place again?" he asked.

"Yes," I said. "Yes, I am."

He dialed, then pointed to a phone on a table nearby and said, "Talk."

I kept watching him as I picked up the phone. I was sure that he was suspicious.

Taher answered again. "We have been waiting for your

call," he said. "You can talk with the pastor. I am going to contact him, but, unfortunately, he just got a call and you will be on hold for a little bit. If his call takes too long, then we will call you back at the number you called from. We saved it here."

I was kept on hold until my minutes finished. I paid the operator, then sat down to wait. I waited and waited but got no call.

Back at my uncle's shop, thoughts rushed through my mind. I worried that if the radio station finally called back, and the PCO operator answered the phone, he would get all the information. I was counting the minutes.

Fifteen minutes later, the PCO agent's nephew ran after me, and he asked in front of my uncle and my dad, "Who is Atal?"

My uncle answered, "This is Atal. What's happened?"

The nephew said, "There is a call from Taher." When he said these words, I looked from side to side. I was seated at a table with my uncle on my right, my father on my left, and neighbors in the other seats.

Everybody exclaimed, "Calling for him? Taher? He keeps doing his old business! He is an agent!"

As I got up to leave, Uncle Amanullah slapped my back. "Who is calling you?" he demanded. "You keep having these conversations?"

He and Sater escorted me to the PCO, holding me by my wrists. It took us ten minutes to get to the PCO and by then, I had missed my call. They asked the operator who had called for me.

The operator, a native Pakistani who had a powerful family in the area, said, "I listened to his conversations and recorded them. I knew where that number was from. He is talking to the company that teaches Christianity. They want to create a Christian community here. You need to make him talk more, so I can figure out more details."

In front of my uncle and my cousin, the agent held me by my neck, slapped me in my face, and pushed me. "This is Pashtun country. Millions of people have come here to change our beliefs and traditions, but they have not succeeded. They were killed here. Who are you? Where do you get support from?"

"I don't get any support!" I said. "I was just interested in getting a job there. If I could work at the radio station" He pushed on my neck so hard I could hardly breathe.

"I know your uncles," he said, "and I am sure that they can take care of everything. I will give you a warning. I can find your group of people who are helping you, and I am watching you." He pointed to my uncle and said, "You know my job here. Our community is huge. If I call people now, they will shoot you dead right here. You are not to let this guy have any more contact with them. I have heard what this guy has been doing in our community, and now I have seen his face. God has helped me by bringing him to my door."

He slapped me in my face again. "We will decide what to do with him in the future. Get out!"

As we left, my uncle tried to explain the situation and reaffirm that nobody was conspiring with me, that I was doing all this by myself. He explained that I was not listening to him or the family. He described to him how they had beaten me badly time after time and that they had given me a lot of warnings. He explained that I hadn't had any contact with the radio station for many years because they had kept a constant vigil on me and all my belongings.

"This is a big embarrassment to us," my uncle said. "He is bringing us shame. Please do not tell anybody. Let us deal with him in a different way. You know my family. We are refugees here. Please, be a little patient. Give us a little more time."

We returned to Uncle Amanullah's shop. Satar said to Amanullah and my father, "Leave it to us. We will take care of him." He was referring to his brothers and cousins.

My family took me home, and for the second time, they started attacking Seema and Maryam. They kept shouting at us and beating us. They were saying that Seema and Maryam must not support me. Now, that the community leader knew about me, our situation was more dangerous. The family was terrified.

Several families met to discuss how to handle the situation. Leaving the area was suggested. At first, the relatives in the city said they would not move; their shop was successful, and my young cousins were busy with their jobs. Soon, however, they changed their minds because the turmoil I had caused would affect their business. No one wanted to associate with us in any way.

Looking for a new place to live took many months, and in the meantime there was no friendly environment for me. Everybody refused to talk to me. They warned Seema and Maryam to avoid me or risk being killed by their own family members. We all were afraid that somebody might attack us, possibly inside our home. Day and night we were vigilant, and the men kept their guns by their sides as they slept.

One evening, I overheard a conversation among my young cousins. "You do not have to fight with anybody. The solution to our problem is simple. We can just kill Atal."

Another said, "Then our family will live in peace. We will not have any more embarrassment for the family."

That's how they thought.

My parents and sister were distraught. I was their youngest child and baby brother. Everybody cried and pleaded with me, "Please, you have to stop! This isn't a game. What you are doing is dangerous, and you will be killed! Think of your future! When you complete your education and get your degree, you will be a doctor. You can treat your people with peace and dignity. We are sure people will like you. You have a very soft and pure heart. We know that you have seen many horrors since you were sent away. We know that you completely disagree with the beliefs and culture here. But, you are still too young to judge for yourself. It is not a good time to challenge these people. You know the people in this community have been treating us as outsiders. And now, because of you, we have to leave here. But those people can find us wherever we go. Do you think we will ever be safe? No, not at all."

There were a million words I wanted to say, but because of my respect for my family and their sadness, I said nothing.

Life continued just like this. The family was worried every day from the moment I left the house to go to school until I got back. When I was a little late, they became even more anxious. Sometimes they sent small kids to see if I was coming from school or not. They were extremely worried about me.

Finally, we found a house in Hangu, about 30 miles from the village we were in. We were lucky to find a house in close proximity but enough distance to feel safe. It was in the middle of the fields, on the outskirts of a town consisting of some one thousand families. There were no neighbors around us. The house was not very comfortable, but it had electricity.

Before we moved, the villagers already knew we were going to Hangu.

All of the family, including my immediate family and my uncles and their families, all moved together. Some felt safer because we were secluded, but others worried that if we were attacked no one would ever know or come to our rescue. The family, especially my mother, was still worried about me because the Kahi villagers understood the reason why we left the village. Nonetheless, we started our new life in Hangu.

Chapter 18

Our home was a huge residence. In fact, it was so big that the landlord built a wall in the middle of the yard to make it into two homes. He rented the other half to a family that had five girls, one of whom had been promised in marriage but was never given. Frequently, we would wake up at night to the sound of gun shots. The family to whom the girl had been engaged wanted revenge. However, our new neighbors often told us that they did not know who was coming at night. They said whoever it was seemed to always be at the corner of the house on our side, not theirs.

When bullets flew, my mom and sisters would rush me from my bed to a storage room where the grain for livestock was kept. We were never sure if these attacks were meant for our neighbors or us. In spite of the danger, we felt a little safer having neighbors who were so vigilant in protecting the property. In fact, the mother and her three oldest girls were very adept at shooting Kalashnikov rifles, and kept quite an arsenal for their protection. They even lent five of their Kalashnikovs to my family.

Maryam was able to start going to a religious homeschool again after a four-year absence. She was still the best in her group. She won a lot of prizes and recognition from the village, and people were always surprised by her ability to learn. Friends of my family often came out from the village of Kahi to our home in Hangu. Everything was going well. We could pay our rent and electric bills. Still, my family felt the rent was too high and blamed me. "All these problems are because of you," they said.

A short time later, Uncle Manan left us and took his family back to live in Afghanistan. Before he left, he told me that I should move as far away as I could. I was never sure if he was concerned for my safety or just wanted me to be out of the family. That was in 2001. Our families were divided.

We began to attend the mosque that was close to our new home. It was a huge mosque with about three hundred members. We soon learned that the people here held the same beliefs as the people back in Kahi. At that time the Taliban were in control of that part of Pakistan. The mosque had a school to train Taliban soldiers for Jihad, and the mullahs "educated" the students about non-Muslim people. My father was in total disagreement with that. He tried to keep the mosque as a place for people to pray.

In 2002, the leaders of the mosque found out that we had been recent refugees, so my father had a lot of arguments with them. They ordered, "You must not come to the mosque.

We know all about your son." They uttered disrespectful words in front of my family and said that we did not follow the law. My family became so concerned about me that I could not go outside in the evening, and I was forbidden to wander far off from our home.

Over time I learned about the climate of this area. The Taliban had run for their lives from Afghanistan and taken over here. They closed city shops and TV stores. They made sure no one was wearing Western-style clothes and that women were kept indoors. The people in the area welcomed them and brought them cows, food and supplies to support them in their effort to return to Afghanistan to fight the U.S. The Taliban and religious schools came out in cars with huge speakers and drove all around, broadcasting their messages.

"Please come and help us support our brave fighters. Support does not have to be only money. Bring your gold! Bring your animals!" They drove by many times a day. People offered whatever they had to show their support.

On the bright side, Maryam was studying religion. There were two teachers who taught eighty girls. The area was not safe enough for Maryam to go to homeschool by herself. I accompanied her until she met with a group of students who walked together.

There was also talk about Maryam's upcoming marriage. Seven years had passed and although no one ever wanted to think about it, in hushed tones some of the women began whispering. I hatched a plan to save five hundred rupees so that Maryam and I could run away. But could we really do this? What chance would we have? I knew we could get a head start. Instead of going to school, we could take a bus to another city, then another city, until we were far away. Then, I could call the radio station, and they could help us. But would they? Could they? What would happen if we got stopped? Would they bring us back? Would they decide to kill Maryam? And did I know her life would be so bad? Was it too risky?

I went back and forth with my ideas again and again. She could die if my plan failed. And I wasn't sure if Maryam would even want to run away — she still didn't even know that she was engaged. I continued saving my rupees and figured I could wait to decide after I met her fiancé. Maybe he would be suitable for her.

In 2003, after Maryam turned fourteen years old, her future husband's family came to our house. With them, of course, was Shah, her fiancé. He was, in everyone's opinion, quite handsome — tall and light-skinned with big, green eyes and a friendly smile. But he also had brown-stained teeth and a constant cough, and though he didn't look it, the family all knew he was addicted to heroin. We also knew he couldn't keep a steady job. We had heard about arguments he had with his family and stories that he had been stealing to support his habit. And yet we needed to decide who it would be to tell Maryam this was going to be the man she would have to spend the rest of her life with. Nobody had the courage to tell her that she was engaged and in only a few days she would be married. She would not be able to see her family or finish school.

Everybody had always treated Maryam like a princess. She was one of the cutest girls in the family. Now nobody could muster the courage to look in her eyes and tell her that she should put henna on her hands. The whole family was agitated; nobody had agreed with her engagement in the beginning, and nobody agreed with her wedding now. That is, except her father. I did not respect him because of this decision. I hoped there would be a court or judge that could take that kind of person and put him in prison for destroying another's dreams.

That was the saddest time of my life and my family's life, too, for we knew Maryam's fate.

Everybody was preparing for a wedding party, but Maryam's family let her believe it was her brother's wedding. Nobody was happy. I prayed every day to God that something would change, and Maryam would not get married.

Maryam was still going to school. On the day the guests arrived, she prepared her books and said, "Today, I will just go to school and ask my teachers if I can miss three days for my brother's wedding. I will come back very soon." The words were so sweet that I was not able to control my tears. I tried to hide them from Maryam, but she saw. She asked, "Why are you crying?"

"You are amazing," I said. "Look, the family is very busy with the wedding party, but you are still achieving your goal. You are still studying. You are doing great. This is good."

"You scared me," she said. "I thought something bad happened to you. It is okay. You already missed two days. You should go and tell your teachers that you will miss two more. Take your books and go." I had no energy to say anything. My sadness was overwhelming.

Maryam went, but she came back soon, crying. I asked her if she was okay. She said, "Yes, I'm okay. But as I was leaving school, most of my classmates looked very sad, and my teachers hugged me like I was going on a very long trip and not coming back. The family looks so worried. I still do not understand what is going on. Why aren't they happy about the wedding?"

I lied to her that it was because the groom, Hamid, was

not here. He was still working in a different country. This wedding would take place in a couple of days "long distance" for him. He would not take part.

When she went to her room, I followed. I wanted to spend as much time with her as I could and keep her happy, but Maryam was very uneasy. I saw the worry on her face, and she did not want to talk to me, but somehow she was still smiling. I complained that I was so tired from making all the wedding arrangements. Decorating, shopping, bringing supplies! She said, "I feel bad for you. You do everything. It is very hard."

We were in the middle of this conversation when Uncle Manan, who was visiting for the wedding, entered the room. "I want to talk to you for a minute," he said to Maryam. "You know in our culture girls do not stay in their parents' home forever. We did not tell you seven years ago that you were engaged to Shah. Now is the time for you to prepare yourself for the wedding."

I learned later that Uncle Manan had volunteered to tell Maryam because no one else wanted to. They couldn't even be in the same room when he delivered the news. Maryam was shocked and started to cry. But she understood there was no choice but to accept what her family had decided for her.

When my uncle left, I quickly approached Maryam. I just put my hands on her shoulders, and she said, "You are my best friend. Why didn't you tell me before? Why were you dishonest with me?" I had no answer to her questions.

I put my hand in the pocket of my Shart, removed the one-hundred-sixty-five rupees I had saved so far for our escape and put them in her small hand.

"It's your decision now," I said. "I am ready to run away with you."

"In a thousand years, no girl in my family has ever run away. I'm not going to bring shame to my family like that. No, I can't do it. We will die."

I said, "I will always be on your side. I am sorry, but I cannot do anything if you choose to stay. Let's prepare you for the wedding that our God has decided for you then. Be patient." With that, I left the room.

I tried to hold my tears back, but I could not. My feelings hurt so bad. Maryam was not just my cousin; she was my closest friend. She had defended me and kept so many of my secrets to keep me safe. Now, I was losing my best friend.

The following day, her fiancé's people came to get the bride, but they were going to stay for two days because they had come such a long distance. Maryam's wedding started, and the designated people from our family prepared to leave for the trip to another city to get her brother Hamid's bride for the second wedding, my other cousin's wedding. They encouraged me, "Come with us." But I said, "No, I want to stay here with Maryam." Two days into the wedding celebration Maryam still was not in a festive mood.

Shah's family shared with our family their hope his new wife would help him to stop using drugs. He had not been normal from childhood, they said, and they hoped Maryam would change him. "My cousin is not a doctor," I said. "Who will take care of Maryam if she takes care of your son?" Their plan was not even possible; in the Pashtonwali community, women are not allowed to say anything to their husbands. The situation was getting more complicated, and I was becoming more enraged, but I had no power to change anything. I only had words, but nobody wanted to listen to them.

The day for the second wedding came, and at five in the morning, they had to leave the house and take Maryam to her new home thirteen hours away. She was crying deeply from her heart, and I did the same. I took her hand in the traditional way that brothers and cousins always do. I walked with her to the car where Maryam was supposed to sit. The only words I could say to Maryam were, "Just please be patient. I am always with you."

"Please take care of yourself," she replied. "The area is very dangerous. You are not safe. I will be so worried about you, and I do not know when I will see you next."

I walked far away from the house to a small river. I sat on its bank from morning until afternoon, remembering all the time I had spent with Maryam, our school days together, and the games I played with her. I returned home, and everyone in the house felt the same as I did. My mom was crying, and so were my sister and cousins.

Two days later, Hamid's soon-to-be wife arrived. Hamid was not there, but we had the bride. We enjoyed my cousin's wedding only a little.

Chapter 19

One evening in 2004, someone knocked at the door. I went out and I saw an old man in traditional garb, all in white. He wasn't much taller than me. He wore a small beard, and I guessed his age to be somewhere close to seventy. Still, he appeared to be quite healthy and exuded a feeling of happiness. I said, "Hello, uncle." I called him "uncle" to show respect.

"Is your father at home?" the man asked. "Is his name Turab Khan?

"Yes, who are you?"

"I am Wadaan, a very old friend of your father's. I've been searching for him for two weeks. We worked together some twenty-five years ago, and I haven't seen him in twenty. Just go inside and tell your dad."

"He is not here yet," I replied, "but he will come soon. Please come inside."

He came in. He told me he had traveled a long distance — from England. I excused myself for a moment and rushed to tell my mom. I was so excited to meet this man all the way from England. She prepared tea for us, and I returned to him.

He asked me, "Do you like it here? Why didn't you go to live in a city somewhere? Are you and your family happy here?"

"Cities are not very different," I said. He seemed concerned for us, as if it was obvious to him our lifestyle had changed dramatically. I explained how difficult it was for us to be refugees in Hangu.

"I have some gifts for you and for your dad," he said, opening his travel bag and taking out some shoes and a winter coat. He gave them to me. He said, "I know how bad life is here. Do you see? I have to wear this big turban on my head, so I fit in. Please do not tell anyone that I came from England because people here think that people from other countries have forgotten their religion and culture. But look at you. I am so glad that you have grown up to be such a big man. What grade are you in?"

"I'm in twelfth."

"Okay! I'm going to ask you a question in English." He did, but he understood from the blank look on my face that I had not understood. I told him if he asked me a math question, I could probably answer correctly.

He laughed a little but declined my offer.

I felt so happy speaking with this intelligent, caring and interesting man. This conversation was so different from those I normally had with the village elders, who quizzed me on difficult religious details that no one would know.

Uncle Wadaan listened to me when I spoke, and he said,

"Whatever you are saying and thinking is the truth, but here we are living in the same culture we've been living in for thousands of year so we are behind the New World." I really liked and agreed with what he was saying and wanted the conversation to continue, but by the time he began to explain in detail, everybody had come home.

As my father and Uncle Wadaan greeted each other, they hugged and called each other nicknames from the past.

"You'll never get old!" my father exclaimed.

"But you look so old already living in this place," Wadaan half-heartedly joked. "What's happened to you? How could you have brought your beautiful family to this place in the heart of Taliban after we had fought them for so long? I don't know when you are ever going to wise up. No matter! I apologize for not bringing you a gift, Turab Khan, but I have brought something with me that I think you will be happy to see." With that, he pulled out a wooden chess box.

My father's eyes lit up at the sight of it. I had no idea what it was, but it was clear that it made my father happy.

It turned out that this man and my father worked in the national police together. Uncle Wadaan was a colonel, which was the same rank as my father. He had come here to visit my father and ask him for some help. He wanted to sell his house in Afghanistan. He had bought it twenty-five years earlier.

While we had gone to Pakistan as refugees, he had left for England. Upon his return, the village people who had been occupying it said that his house was not his property anymore. They thought he had been killed in the war. He was very frustrated, and he looked very angry as he spoke because the regime had changed, but the people had not changed. Crime and corruption were very high, he told us. The leaders and their gangs in each city were making their own laws.

As they were catching up on the many years they had been apart, Seema came in to serve them tea. She greeted him, and he guessed, "You must be Turab's daughter. I can see the resemblance."

"Yes," she smiled.

"I am sure there is no place here for you to study, but you can still learn at home. I wish I had been able to bring you some books. Try your best. The situation will improve."

"Thank you for your concern. I am not alone. There are thousands of girls just like me who can't go to school. I try to study, but I also have to help my mother. I clean and cook to help her."

"Speaking of that, I suffer from diabetes. I hope you can take care of me and cook vegetables from your garden for me. There is not a hospital for me to go to if I get sick here."

When I heard that he would stay in our house for a

week, I was very happy.

A couple of days later, my father had to leave the house for a few hours and told me to keep our guest entertained. While Uncle Wadaan and I were sitting in the guest room, he suggested, "Let me show you how to play chess." Until he arrived, I had not seen a chessboard before in my life.

As he was teaching me, he told me, "I knew about your past. Your father told me about some of the difficulty you have had. He told me how you were beaten so many times, and that you have had contact with a radio station. I know you did not mean to do anything bad that could cause your family's reputation to fall. People here can't understand your goals. To explain to these people your interest in learning about another religion and why you were interested in that radio station is pointless. People think that you are an agent or a spy of some sort. That is not very safe for you; it's not even safe in Afghanistan. You know now there is a very huge conflict between Muslims and non-Muslims. Forget about learning about another religion. If they see you with a religious book that is not about Islam, they will shoot you on sight.

"Your father also told me that people are watching you. In fact, your own cousins totally disagree with what you've been doing, and they do not like you. In just these three days

I've been able to see the situation in your house. The way your cousins treat you is very different from how they treat anyone else in the family. They are products of their culture. They want to defend it, not change it. I know you love your family, and you want to live with them, but if your situation starts to become unbearable, I have a friend in Islamabad you can go to for help. He just came here from the United States, and he works for the U.N. You can go to him for advice. He has more education than your father or I do. He has a Ph.D. from a university in the U.S. Try to meet with him. His name is Fazel. I'll give you his address. If your life is in danger, he will be a good person to know."

He wrote Fazel's name and address, which I carefully tucked into my wallet. Then he put some cash in my hand and told me not to tell anyone. I thanked him and put it in my pocket. Later when I was alone, I counted out the money. He had given me fifteen hundred rupees! It was the most money I had ever seen. "If only he had come before Maryam left," I thought as I put the money into my pocket for safe-keeping.

"Use this money for your books, or if you need something," he advised. "I really like you. You are smart, and you have good ideas. I cannot believe that you are an open-minded person in this community. Be safe."

I had a very pleasant time with him. He was the only

person that listened to me and encouraged me in my search for meaning.

The wonderful week filled with happy moments with Uncle Wadaan quickly came to an end. As my father and I walked him to the bus station, he looked worried. He stopped, but his hand on my shoulder and said, "Do not walk with me. It is not safe for you." I reluctantly returned to the house.

The last time Taher called me, in 2004, he told me about a seminar in Islamabad.

"There will be people from different countries attending," he explained. "There will be some people there who know about you, and they are concerned about you. We will give you an award, and you can get it from us there."

The seminar would last three days, but Islamabad was three-hundred-fifty kilometers away from Hangu, which meant I'd be away five days. I thought and thought, but I could not find any reason to explain my absence to my family, and Maryam was not here to help. My sister Seema was sick, and I did not want to trouble her for ideas. I kept it secret. I knew that I was being watched. I knew that some of my relatives kept tabs on me, too, and kept each other informed of my whereabouts. My cousins believed that by killing me they would repair the damage I had caused to the family's reputation, and they were just waiting for an excuse.

What was I going to do about the seminar? I had to think carefully not just about myself but about my parents and sister as well. But after meeting Wadaan, I felt an irrepressible urge to talk with people who understood me.

The day to leave for the seminar came. I told my mom, "I have to go away for several days tomorrow."

She begged me, "Don't do that."

"Mom, everything will be fine. I am going to meet with some good people like Uncle Wadaan."

"This is a bad, bad idea," she countered. "If you go for so many days, people will think that you left and converted to another religion." She asked me not to go, but I had already decided.

I slept poorly that night, then woke up early to a beautiful morning. It was August 19, 2004. After praying alone, I sneaked out of the house with a pen, pencils and paper in a plastic bag. I took a back way to the bus station, hoping no one would see me.

The bus headed out for Peshawar, a three-hour trip. On the way, I noticed the beautiful scenery. So much green! Such a clear blue sky! I noticed the beauty in each river and tree we passed. I had not been that far from home in many years now. This was a good sign that I had made the right decision to go to the conference. Nonetheless, I felt very wary. For the first two hours, I worried that I was being watched. I did not relax until I saw a great deal of traffic and crowds indicating we were near.

I had to change busses to go to Islamabad, my destination, but there was a four-hour wait before its departure. I waited in the bus station with hundreds of people. The smoke from the busses was overwhelming. I wanted to call Taher to let him know I was on my way and which bus I was taking. I found a huge PCO. It was possible to dial the number without an operator's assistance, which was good because I was still worried about being found out. I had heard Peshawar was very dangerous, that the Pashtun people there were very religious. Taliban were there. The biggest *madrasa* in Pakistan was established there. I could be in danger if anyone overheard my plans. Everyone there spoke Pashto and would understand me. I had to proceed with caution.

When I called, Taher answered the phone. "We have been waiting for your call," he said. "We are so glad you made it to Peshawar. When you get to Islamabad, I will be at the bus station with a white car, and I will find you there." I was both excited and worried.

The bus pulled into the Islamabad station around four o'clock. Police officers came to check everybody's ID. I only had my school card. They told me, "You do not have documents. We will take you to the police station." Now, I was in trouble again.

While they checked my pockets and bag as if I were a criminal, I saw the white car Taher had told me about. There were two men inside. One was dressed as a typical Pashtun. The other man, who had red hair and green eyes, was dressed as a Westerner. They walked up to us and asked me, "Are you Atal?" I responded with relief, "Yes." He turned to the police officer and put a hundred rupees in his hand and told him, "This is our person. He is our guest." When the police officer saw the money, there was a big smile on his face. He said, "Wherever you are going, you are free." He looked at me and said, "Sorry." I was surprised and happy.

Taher turned to me and gave me a hug. He said, "You are a very brave person! I am proud of you. We are so happy that you will participate in this seminar." He introduced me to David, who spoke English. Taher translated for me. Everything they said was very encouraging. From there they took me to a hotel called Green Park. Inside was a beautifully landscaped courtyard with a garden, palm trees, and a fountain. In my room, there was a huge bed, a bathroom, and a big TV. I hadn't seen a TV in fifteen years!

"Whatever you need, you can call room service," Taher said, then showed me how to use the phone. "Do this, and you will have food. Enjoy yourself, and get some rest. Tomorrow we will come at eight to pick you up. The seminar will start at nine in the morning."

I spent the evening watching TV. There were many channels to choose from. I liked everything even though I did not recognize any of the actors.

The next morning at the seminar, I saw a lot of people from different countries. The conference consisted of about thirty people, including the pastors who were running it. The pastors were from England, Australia, and Canada, and the participants were Pakistani and Pashtun. They looked to me like most religious people in Pakistan, with their beards and religious beads in traditional *shalwar,* clothes. I was the only Afghani and the youngest person there. Taher introduced me as a special guest, and they welcomed me.

The first seminar started with a reading from the Bible. The facilitators spoke in English, and translators were provided, so everyone could understand. During the first seminar, everyone introduced themselves and shared something about their concerns. The Pakistanis were not very nice to me. They didn't pay attention when it was my turn to talk. Because of the negativity in their words about the seminar, I understood they were not really open-minded people. In fact, they were praying in a way which I did not know.

At the end of the preaching and speeches, the guests started conversing with pastors and there were disagreements about culture and religion. I was so surprised. If these people did not believe in this religion, why were they participating in the seminar?

At the end of the day, I found a comfortable seat in the lobby with a great view of the fountain. I sat and thought about what I had learned. I was still wondering about the Pakistanis.

I was in the middle of my thoughts when two people from the seminar came and stood on my right and left sides. They asked, "Where are you from?" I replied, "I am from Afghanistan." They started asking questions. I really did not want to talk about my personal life and how I contacted the radio. Most of my answers were simply yes and no. I was sure that they worked with another Islamic group and did not feel that I was safe.

They told me, "At the end of this seminar, those British pastors will have some cash money to help people who participated in this seminar. Ask them for a lot of money because you traveled to get here. They will give it to you. We are here to get information and money." It was so strange to me to hear them say that. I had not thought about getting any financial support. My goal was to meet people and learn how to cope with the people where I lived. I was also planning to ask someone if I could work at the radio station.

However, there was no opportunity for me to converse with anyone. There was nothing beside speeches and preaching and teaching the Bible every day. Besides, the Pakistanis were keeping a close watch on me. I knew I had to be careful.

The conference was a great opportunity to compare what I was learning about Christianity with what I had been learning about Islam all my life. I perceived there was a lot of freedom for women in their religion. I was interested in that. But every day the conference began and ended at the same time with seminar after seminar, and little by little I wanted to attend less and stay in my room more. As I learned more about the others who had come, I felt less safe. I found the conference to be so interesting and inspiring, but I began to realize that I was the only person who had come here to learn. Everyone else was there only for money.

At the end of the conference, the distribution of this money caused quite a furor. Although the facilitators had set up a table and expected everyone to wait in line, almost everyone surrounded the table to demand money. If one of the pastors offered a person five hundred rupees the recipient would ask for more, much more. Several of the men shouted to ask for thousands each. They were taking the money, stuffing it in their pockets and then returning to the front of the table to ask for more. I had never been to a conference before, but this did not look normal to me. It looked like stealing. It seemed so disrespectful.

When everyone else had left, one of the pastors called me up to the table. Being the youngest and so shy, I had stayed back and watched. He put his hand on my shoulder and said something. I answered that I could not understand, so a translator was called over. With the help of the translator, I introduced myself and explained that I was an Afghani refugee going to school, and that I had come a long way for the conference.

They offered to give me some travel money. "My goal was not to come for money," I said. "I came here to learn. Please donate that money to someone who needs it more than I do."

They were so surprised!

"We didn't know you were from Afghanistan or that you were a refugee," said Pastor David. "We are so glad you have come here to learn and not for the money. I am very proud of you for that. Still I want to give you something that you can use to buy books for school." With that, he put some money into my hand.

I took the opportunity to share my situation. I told them

about the difficulties that people have in the Pashtun area where the refugees were living in Pakistan. I explained the repercussions of anyone seeing me a hold a Bible. Two of them held my hands while others put their hands on my shoulders and they prayed. I couldn't understand what they were saying, and it was not a real solution. It seemed that they were totally ignorant of anything I described. It might have been because of the translator, or they might not have been educated about it.

"Stay strong!" Pastor David said. "You may establish a church in your area and become a pastor like me someday." I felt dejected. I knew in my heart they meant well, but I also knew they were ill-equipped to advise me. But I had learned the Ten Commandments and so I tried to be patient and respectful.

I was supposed to leave at nine the next morning, but for my protection the conference organizers held me for one more day. They sent me to the bus station by car, the same way I had arrived. I went back to to my city by way of Peshawar. During the journey, I worried about what to tell my family. I wanted to be honest because I believed that people would forgive me if I was honest.

By the time I began to walk from the bus station to my house, it was about four o'clock in the afternoon. I was happy and worried at the same time. I didn't fear telling my family the truth, but I was worried about what would happen to them if other people found out about my trip.

When I reached the gate of my home, I was very tired from the trip and very hungry. The door opened, and my sister and mother came running toward me, crying. They held me in the corner next to the door. I was astonished. I asked, "Is everything okay? What's happened?"

"Nothing is okay!" my mother wailed. "You went to that seminar. That was such a bad idea! Now everyone believes you converted to Christianity. They believe that the people who converted you took a Koran, put it on the ground, and had you stand on it. The whole family's already decided to kill you. Your cousins, your uncles, every one is convinced that killing you will send them to heaven."

"Relax, Mom," I said. "Everything will be okay. Don't be upset! I'm so hungry. Let's go. I haven't eaten the whole day. Can you prepare me something to eat?"

Just then my aunts and cousin joined us. One of them said, "You must leave here immediately. Please, do not stay here. Just run."

My mother handed me a plastic bag with my clothes and school supplies in it, and some money. Later, I wondered if she had sold her very old gold rings to the neighbors to get this money for me. After my ten-hour trip I just wanted to eat and rest, but they wouldn't let me stay. They were all talking at once, pleading with me.

"You must leave now," they said. "They are looking for you. They already spread word to people in the village. Just go and do not come back. Go far where you have friends." They pushed me from the door. "Run! Move fast! Somebody's going to see you!"

But where could I go? I began to walk along the road. I so much wanted to be with my family, and to negotiate with these people more and resolve the conflicts. I thought to myself, "If I do not deal with this issue, and if I leave here, who will bring peace?" On the other hand, I truly did not want my mom or my sister to be hurt because of me. I could not go back. That was a devastating realization for me. I walked along the road and stood for a little while. Should I go to the west side or east side? North or south? I had no idea.

I stopped and sat. I felt like I was dreaming. How did it come to this? Finally, I decided to go to Peshawar. It was a huge city, and my relatives would not be able to find me there.

Chapter 20

After four hours riding on a bus, I arrived in the late evening. I walked until I found a hotel and asked the manager if there was a room. He asked me for my ID. I said that I didn't have any. He said, "You are not allowed to stay in a hotel without an ID. We can't trust you. You might come here to commit a crime."

I left and walked to different hotels, but all of them had the same rule. What was I going to do? I was afraid of the police. If they caught me, they could take me to jail. I walked through a city park. It was past midnight and I could only keep moving since there was nowhere to rest. I was lucky I did not see a police officer. I was also lucky that it was August and the weather was warm. My night ended without a bit of sleep.

With no other choice I called Taher at the radio station and I told him my situation. He told me, "You're back here? I'm sorry, but we cannot give you a place to live here. I suggest you return home. I'll discuss this with my co-workers and our president."

Return home? I was very disappointed. I had been sure they were going to help me, but clearly they did not understand my situation at all.

I remembered my mom telling me about some distant

relatives, the Mirwises, who had left Kabul and moved to Peshawar. They had probably been here for ten years. I decided to find them, but it was not going to be an easy task. All I knew was that they lived in the section of the city called Sadar. Most people there were rich. It was located very close to Khaybar Pashtunistan, an area with no government, an independent place where many religious leaders and drug dealers lived. But I didn't know this at the time.

I made my plan. The area was divided into territories called phases. There were a thousand houses in each phase. I decided to search for them phase by phase. The phases were modern, with paved streets and a market area lined with small, colorful shops. Vendors had fresh fruit and other produce out front displayed on wooden wagons. This is where I would search for them.

I took a bus to Phase Three and searched the market area. I looked in each shop in order to find an Afghani shopkeeper who might know the family. But I had no luck. I also had the same problem finding a hotel, so I spent the night in a park.

The next day, still wearing the same clothes I had been wearing when I fled my home, I found a restaurant in a dirty area. I had a small dinner of leftovers from the restaurant, a cold mix of rice, a little beef and chickpeas. I was so hungry

285

that I ate it very quickly. The workers stared at me. The cashier was very old and spoke to me in my native language. I told him, "I have been here in this city, but there is no place to sleep. I am afraid the police might catch me. I have no documents. I am a student." He listened to me and said, "Our restaurant's second floor is the place where workers sleep. I can give you a space in a room there. I will charge you thirty rupees per night." He called another worker to show me the bed. It was in a very messy place with a lot of flies. There were eight more beds. They were very smelly. Some workers were sleeping there. I decided I could stay here until I found my relatives' house. There was no other choice. I really appreciated the room. I told him, "Okay, I will be here at night. I am not sure how long I will stay here."

A couple of the workers were smoking hashish. "Welcome!" they said. "Join us! Smoke some of this. It will make you happy."

"Thank you, but no," I declined.

The city was not safe for me at that age. Sometimes, people in the city attacked boys and girls for sex. I didn't know this at the time; no one ever spoke about it. But I was concerned about where I was staying. Each night as I lay down to sleep, I clutched with one hand the pocket where my Bible verses were kept to ensure they stayed hidden away. With the other hand I covered a secret pocket my mom had sewn for money to be sure no one attempted to search me as I lay sleeping.

One night during my stay at the so-called "hotel," everyone was talking, so I couldn't fall asleep. A girl maybe twenty years old entered and sat down on the floor. I wondered if she was a worker at the restaurant. It was highly unusual to find a woman working at a restaurant, but why else would she be here? The workers started to collect money among themselves. I overheard their conversation. She said, "My mother is very sick. I have no other way to get the money we need for her."

"If I don't eat tomorrow, I can give her some money," I thought. I quietly reached for 20 rupees and passed them to one of the workers to give to her.

When all the money was collected from the workers, they took her to a corner of the room, and one by one they had sex with her. I was so shocked! One of them men called to me, "If you have fifty rupees, you can have sex with this girl. It is okay, if you don't have money, you can do it for free. You're a special guest. You even look different. Maybe you are a virgin. You should try her!"

I replied, "In my religion and in my family they did not

teach me such things. I am not interested."

They laughed. Another worker said, "If you don't want to join in, then leave the place for a couple hours. Let us enjoy ourselves. You are the most boring person."

I felt so bad for the girl. I could hear her screams. I wanted to tell her, "You don't have to have sex with them. I have some money; I can help you." But the workers were angry that I wasn't joining them, and kept shouting at me. I got up and left, relieved to get out of there. I walked outside until two in the morning.

Finally, after a week of searching, I found a shopkeeper, Abdullah, in Phase Two, who said he could help me find Mirwise. He gave me some tea and pastry and promised to take me at the end of the day, when he closed his shop.

There were parks and huge gardens of oranges and other fruit nearby. I walked to the fields, counting the hours to go back to the shopkeeper and finally go to my relatives' house. There was no promise that I could find them, but I was hopeful. Finally, the day came to an end. The shopkeeper said, "Just wait for two more hours, and we can go together." He gave me some water, and I waited there.

After two more hours of waiting, we took a bus. It took about twenty minutes. He asked some people at the market about Mirwise. One man said, "I believe we know a man by this name. You can find him at the next market. You do not have to take the bus. You can walk from here."

As we walked we asked some boys about the family. One of them knew Mirwise. He led us to another shopkeeper, who knew where the family's house was. "It is on First Street," he said. Those were the happiest words I'd heard in a long, long time. "Thank God!" I said, then looked at myself. My clothes were filthy. As I realized that I'd been wearing them for ten days, my joy turned to fear of rejection.

We reached the home and knocked at the gate. Mirwise opened the door and looked at me. He said, "How can I help you? Do you need some food?"

Abdullah smiled, "No, this is one of your relatives. He has been looking for you for about ten days. Hopefully, you can help him. I've done all I can do."

"I am Turab Khan's son," I said. Mirwise's expression of puzzlement changed to surprise, and he hugged me.

"I haven't seen you for a very long time!" he said. "You were only two years old. Now look at you! You're a grown man! We used to call you Tur." (This nickname came from my grandfather. He had called me *Tur* after the black and brown bee that he said I resembled when I was very small.) "You still look like your father." He led me into the house. He called for

289

his wife and children to join us. He addressed them, "Do you know who this is?"

His wife was hurriedly trying to shut the door. As was the custom when guests came, women tried to hide from sight. He called out, "It's okay. Come here. This is not a guest. It is Tur."

"Really?" his wife asked. She ran to greet me, and with one look at me insisted, "Run to the bathroom and take a shower. I will bring you clean clothes." She brought me a towel and I went to clean up.

After my shower, I joined them in the room where everyone would eventually go to sleep. They were so happy to see me and welcomed me as if I were one of their own. They asked how my family was doing. Mirwise's wife, Ziba, said, "Your family helped us a lot. After you were sent to live in your grandmother's village, our house was destroyed in the war. Our clothes and all of our belongings were stolen. We had to run for our lives without anything. Thank God your family was there to help us. We moved to your father's house. It was a wonderful experience to be with them. I will always remember how they took such good care of us. We stayed with them for almost two years. They shared all their food with us. Our kids were very happy there."

I learned that Mirwise had been injured in the war. He was not able to work, and relied on support from his wife's family in Germany. But they recounted the many happy memories they had with my sisters even though the city was embroiled in war.

Because of all they shared with me, I had confidence to tell them, "I am not a one-night guest. I am not able to go back to my family." I told them a few details about my difficulty living there. Ziba reassured me, "This is your house. This is your family. Feel free. Whatever you need, you can take it for yourself because your family did so much for us."

"Your family did not just help us," Mirwise said. "When you were not yet born, your family chose my wife Ziba, and I have had the best life with her. It is because your family chose her for me. But let's talk about the details later. You must be hungry."

Ziba gave me something to eat. I was so thankful for it. I couldn't remember when I wasn't hungry. Knowing I had somewhere to stay, my appetite came back, and I started eating like a crazy man. Everything was delicious.

I saw a lot of books around. Their five kids were studying. All of them were in school. While I was eating, I saw that two sons, Rafiq and Ahmad, were having difficulty with their math. They were squabbling, saying, "You don't know anything," and the other one was saying, "No, you do not know."

I sat down with them and offered to help. They looked at me and asked, "Do you know math?"

"A little bit," I said. Ahmad showed me his homework and I was able to solve the problems. I also helped Rafiq. They were so excited. "You know everything!" exclaimed Ahmad. They ran to tell their sisters. Soon the three sisters, Mina, Zarka, and Sharina, came with their books and notebooks and said, "We also need help in math."

I helped them do their homework and little by little, they became comfortable with me. It made me think about my own situation. I was still one year away from graduating from high school. How lucky I was that my sister and mom had thought to pack all of my school records.

I continued to help the kids late into the night. It was almost three in the morning when we finally went to sleep. When we woke up, they went to school, and I stayed by myself. Their parents thanked me for helping the kids the night before.

Now that we were alone, Mirwise, Ziba, and I could talk.

"People were trying to kill me," I told them, and explained some of the story about the radio station. "Don't worry. I will not say anything to your family about it. Can I ask you to not tell them either? I would not want to bring any harm to them. Maybe your kids would tell their classmates if they knew. Let's keep everything secret."

"Does anybody know that you have come here?" Mirwise asked.

"Only God knows," I assured him. "Let's keep it between us. The people who want to hurt me can find this place. I don't want your family to be in danger. Believe me! I will not do anything that will affect your life negatively. I'll be like one of your kids. I really need your help to get into a school to finish my high school education."

"We will help you," Mirwise said. "We are so glad that you are a survivor. You don't have to worry. If you are in danger, we are here for you. You are now part of our family."

Still, Ziba was worried about her kids; she didn't want her daughters to be in a dangerous situation. By the time we finished talking, it was around two o'clock in the afternoon. The children arrived home from school, happy and excited.

They boasted, "Our homework was the best. We even did a couple of the problems that Atal helped us with on the board! The whole class applauded!" Their dad was so happy. Their mother thanked me.

The next day, Mirwise took me to a school to ask for

admission. The security guard asked us, "What do you need here?"

"We need to get admission for my nephew," Mirwise answered him.

"It seems to me that you are a refugee."

"Yes."

"There is no admission for refugees."

Mirwise told him, "You are a security guard. This is not your job. Let us go inside."

"If you give me some money, then I will let you go inside," he said. Tired of standing in front of the school door, I took twenty rupees from my pocket and put them into his hand. He said, "All the school is yours. Go ahead."

We headed to the principal's office. We knocked on the door, and the principal said, "I will get back to you. You can wait here." After keeping us waiting two hours, he said the school did not admit refugees.

We went to one school after the other, but all of them rejected me because I was not native-born. After meeting some local people who had a good deal of knowledge of the area, they showed me some other schools where I might be accepted. We finally found a school run by Afghanis, Taqwa High School. Its student body was made up of Afghani students. The school environment was not that different from what I had experienced in Kahi and Hangu. The students there still believed in religion more than technology, but I was happy.

Things were looking up for another reason too. David, whom I had met at the conference in Islamabad, was in Peshawar.

He was the director of the *Good News for All* radio program and was also was responsible for the Peshawar Church. It was a very small red brick church and with a cross on top, in a secret place near the edge of an old part of the city.

I called Pastor David from a public phone one day, and he invited me to his house for lunch. A Canadian, he'd learned to speak Pashto after sixteen years in Peshawar where he had been working as a professor. His original job and that of some of his close friends was pastor. I began meeting with him on a regular basis and attending the church. I also began to go to the *Good News for All* Agency for Bible study.

David was responsible for the whole Bible study agency in Peshawar and I met some professors working there too. One of them was Tom. He was a math instructor. He said, "If you need some help after school, I can help you improve your math and physics skills. And if you have chemistry problems, I can help you with them, too." That was good news for me.

Tom lived in a huge house. I went there often for tutoring. I'd spend about two hours each visit. He spent half an hour teaching me math. The remainder of the time, he taught me Bible verses. All of the church and agency members got together at Easter, Christmas, and other holidays.

Along with going to school and meeting at Tom's house to learn math, I was helping Mirwise's children with their schooling. When their classmates saw that their grades were improving and they were getting better at school, some of the families were interested in me teaching their children. A family that lived nearby offered to hire me, and I eagerly agreed. I went there five days a week.

My own grades were very good. Tom's help was making a great difference. My classmates often asked me, "Where did you come from?" But I did not want to talk about my past. It was not safe to even talk about Tom's tutoring.

A month after tutoring for the first family, a couple more families approached me to tutor their children. I agreed. Mirwise's family could not support me. For my books, supplies and school tuition, I had to work.

All was going very well in my life. I was excelling in school, being tutored, and tutoring others to bring in some much-needed money. Sometimes, David and Tom invited me to meet with them, and they told my story to people who visited from the United States, Canada, and Australia. But they kept most of their activities secret because the area was becoming more radical every day. This small group of Christians was surrounded by a huge community that did not want them there. They did not know whom they could trust.

Chapter 21

By the end of 2004, it was commonly believed that Christians had something to do with removing the Taliban from power. The Pashtuns here believed that the conflict was between Muslims and Christians, not NATO and Afghanistan. They believed that Christians were coming here to Pakistan to remove the mullahs and put pastors in the mosques. In their sermons at the mosques, they encouraged people not to accept any help from Christians and not to listen to them. They asserted that it was the time for *jihad*. They collected money to support the Taliban in regaining control of Afghanistan, which they described as a province of Pakistan.

Thousands of villagers opened their doors to the Taliban and supported them financially. Loudspeakers were set up on tables along the roads to relay their propaganda. "People, now is the time for *jihad*. Bring your support here to help in the fight against non-Muslim people. They will destroy our religion and culture. It is time to help the fighters." People brought money. Women brought gold jewelry. People who had no money brought their sheep and goats. The tension was getting worse and worse.

The church secretly celebrated Christmas 2004 in the basement of Tom's house. Everybody was told to come alone, not in groups. We had a lot of fun. Tom was a great host.

In the new year I kept going to school, tutoring and getting private lessons to work on my skills. I was very interested in science. But Mirwise's family was worried about the growing tensions. They advised me not to walk around the city. It was becoming dangerous, and I was not really very far from Hangu.

In fall 2005, a Danish magazine published an offensive cartoon of Prophet Mohammed. Angry people, encouraged by mullahs, rioted. They burned stores and cars. A local KFC was burned and the workers were killed. The situation was bad for almost a month. The radio office and church were attacked, but it was stopped by the police.

Letters warning and threatening the Christians were sent. They stopped assembling together at the church, and met at each other's houses instead. I was told to be very careful if I wanted to meet with them. "Do not use only one way to come here," I was advised. "Try to change your routes each time you visit." They suggested keeping in contact by phone, but only if it was important. Most of their friends moved from the city, but David, Taher, and Shams stayed in Peshawar. We got together sometimes to share crucial information.

In 2006, a pastor from the southern United States

burned a Koran, leading to more violence in Peshawar. On a Friday, we got together for a meeting, but this time, David decided to meet at the office. He did not want to jeopardize his children's safety by meeting at his home. During the meeting, an angry mob hit the streets and burned down a lot of shops. We were informed by phone that they were headed in our direction.

The mob was much bigger, louder and angrier than the previous year. This time, the police were not able to control the crowds. They climbed over the outside walls, broke the metal gates, and tore down the walls and climbed to the roof to get inside.

I made my way outside, I turned around to look at the little brick church. On the roof, I saw protesters trying to tear off the metal cross by rocking it back and forth. Suddenly, I thought that I would be better off on the street on my own. I and ran and ran until, finally, I reached a place far from the rioting. Then I headed home. It took about four hours on foot.

The next day, I tried to call Shams and Taher, but nobody answered. I kept trying, but they did not respond. Then I tried David, and he explained what had happened. "The office is closed," he said. " Some of the members have been kidnapped. Hopefully, they are okay. If we get anymore information, I will let you know."

I waited three days, then called David again. He told me, "You must not use anybody's phone, it could put our lives in danger. Our conversation might be recorded. I can only tell you that Shams was kidnapped and killed. Taher was injured and remains in the hospital. As I told you when we last spoke, the office is totally destroyed. We will not be able to meet our members or guests. We hope the situation will improve, but I will not be here much longer. I am leaving the city."

The news of Shams' death tore at me. I liked him. We had many good memories from the many events we shared. I considered him a true friend.

Most people associated with the church left the city. I was not able to meet with any of them. I could not reach out to anyone for help. The situation around the area was very dangerous, and Mirwise was growing uncomfortable with my living at his house. He began to realize that my tutor Tom had not only been teaching me math. I learned that more relatives were coming, bringing someone to Peshawar for a hospital visit, and they knew my family. When they learned who I was, word could get back to Hangu, and I could be found out. I sensed that I had overstayed my welcome. It was time for me to go. But go where?

I remembered that my father's friend from England,

Wadaan, had advised me to reach out to his cousin Fazel, the United Nations worker, if I ever needed help. Maybe he could tell me what to do. Finally, after determining the logistics, I reached the decision to go to Islamabad to find Fazel. I had to ride several buses to get there.

When I arrived in Islamabad, I was able to get a hotel room with my student ID card and Afghani security papers. Early the next morning, I took a taxi to Fazel's office. The building was under very high security and nobody was allowed to enter without a full security check. With much begging, I finally convinced them to let me in. But at the security window, the officer shouted, "Out! Leave this place immediately."

"Fazel is my relative," I pleaded. "If it is possible, could someone call and ask him if I could meet with him."

"Who sent you here?" he demanded. "Give me your information."

"Please say Wadaan sent me here to meet with him. If he accepts that, then he will tell you to let me in. If not, I will go away. Please tell him. I have spent a lot of money to come here from Peshawar."

He shook his head and agreed.

The security guard called Fazel from the reception window and repeated what I had told him. Then he hung up the phone, turned to me, and said, "Wait here. You might be able to go inside." I was so relieved. A few anxious minutes later, a distinguished-looking man dressed in a handsome dark suit, white Shart and tie walked through the door, and asked the officer, "Where is this person?" The officer pointed at me. He looked at me and said, "Oh! So it is you?" There I stood in my dirty clothes and broken shoes. I must have been quite a sight to him.

Fazel signaled me to come forward, and gave me his hand and a hug. "It is a pleasure to meet you," he said. "Let's go to my office," As we walked, he confirmed that Wadaan had told him about me, but he never expected me to show up at his office one day.

His office was huge and extremely beautiful. He had many secretaries and an enormous number of file cabinets in his office. His workers treated him with a great deal of respect. He offered me tea with some cookies and chocolate. He said, "Sit here and enjoy your tea. I have matters to take care of. We will talk later." He seemed happy to meet me.

I sat there watching in amazement as I enjoyed the tea and cookies. He was very busy. A lot of people came and went, each bringing files. At about two o'clock, we went to his home for lunch. While we were eating at the table in the dining room, he said, "I already know something of your past. How can I help you? Why did you want to meet with me?"

I told him the difficulties that I had been having in Peshawar. I confessed that I did not know what to do with my life or how to get out of the dangerous situation I was in. My cousins or anyone else who wanted to harm me would be able to locate me in Peshawar. Most of the people I knew had either left the city or refused to meet me anymore. I was alone. I asked him for his advice.

He thought for a little bit. He said, "Unfortunately, I cannot offer you a place to live. You cannot stay with me here. I am very busy. I'm an American citizen, so I am also in a bit of a dangerous situation, so it would not be a good idea."

I asked, "Could you please help me get an identification card, so I can live here legally?"

"My job is not related to that. You can fill out an application and give it to United Nations High Commissioner for Refugees, UNHCR. Do you know how to write in English?"

I shook my head no but he continued as if he already knew that I couldn't.

"If you could fill out the application in English, it would be easier for them to process, so I will help you. I'll write a note you can take to the UNHCR to get the application. You must not show this note to anyone." In the note, he introduced me, and included some information about my religious conflict with the Pashtuns and the problems I was having living in

Pakistan illegally.

He explained that it was important that he write a translation in English for me to be sure it was clear when it was reviewed. He folded it, slipped it into a plain white envelope and handed it to me. "You must not lose it, or you will be in greater danger."

I put the envelope into my pocket and thanked him again and again. He instructed me to go to the UNHCR office to get the application. Next, he said to have someone from the Christian agency write a letter to verify that he knew me and knew that I was in trouble. Fazel told me to be extremely cautious.

"Are the people from the Christian community trustworthy people?" he asked.

"They are my good friends," I assured him.

"If they are your good friends, you should be able to stay with them, shouldn't you? Have they ever helped you with any financial support?"

I said, "No."

"Have they ever tried to find you a house or room where you can live?"

"No."

"I know you believe they are your friends," he said. "However, they are working for their agency; they are trying to spread their religion to all the people."

"Yes," I agreed. "I attended one of their seminars to learn about Christianity. They encouraged me to be there and introduced me to the many pastors who had come from all over the world."

"I see," he said slowly. He paused for a moment to choose his words carefully. "These seminars are a show. They want the other pastors to see their progress. Be careful not to be used by them for their own goals. This is no time to be meeting people or trying to make them understand you. They will not understand your goals, and they will not listen to you. The discussion that we are having right now must be secret, and you are not to talk about me, repeat my name or give my address to anyone in any interviews.

"I am proud of you for the courage you have shown. It is not easy to disagree with your family and face so many problems because of your beliefs. Wadaan had told me about your goals, but you cannot pursue them here at this time. Follow through with UNHCR. Here. Take my home telephone number with you. If you have an emergency or if you have a big issue in Peshawar, you can contact me. Be careful." He gave me a hug as I left his residence.

As soon as I left, I headed for the UNHCR office to get the application. There were local Pakistani police officers standing in front of the entrance way. I showed the envelope to them and told them it was my application and that I needed to get inside. An officer with a long beard told me he had to see the application, but I knew that it was not his job to look at it. I tried to slip by them, but the police officer threatened to take me to jail if I didn't show him the application. With no alternative, I opened up the envelope and handed him the note. He and another officer read it.

"Ohh! Your family must be so proud of you," he said sarcastically. "How is it that you are still alive?"

"Okay! You can go in," said the other officer. I was sure from his clean-shaven face and attire that he was not Pashtun.

I submitted my application. The clerk at the desk told me that there was a branch in Peshawar and that I should visit that office because it would be much more convenient for me. Before leaving, I was given a phone number to call in case of emergency.

I started my bus trip back to Peshawar. I thought about how to get the letter I needed from David. For all I knew he had already left the country. But I was sure that because David was British, he would be the best choice to give me the proof I needed.

I called David many times before I finally reached him.

I explained that I really needed to meet with him for a couple of hours because I needed his help with something very urgent. We planned to meet in three days because he was very busy preparing to leave the city. He said he wasn't sure where we'd meet yet, but he would let me know in advance. Three days passed. No word came, so I called him again. He said we could meet for a short time at his new house, which was located among the houses where governmental officials lived.

When we got together, I told him I had written an application for UNHCR. I told him I was trying to get identity papers, so I wouldn't be harassed by the police anymore and could travel more freely. Then I told him I needed a reference letter for UNHCR from him to prove and verify my situation for the past ten years, starting with my letters to the radio station.

Much to my surprise, David refused to write anything for me. He said he thought I should stay in Peshawar because everybody had problems here. He showed me a chapter in the Bible and said that Jesus instructed us to face our difficulties. I had never asked for any help from the radio station group, and I had never accepted any when they offered it to me. I was shocked that now when I needed it most, I was refused. I remembered what Fazel had said. I think David wanted me to remain there so that he would have a contact and be able to use me as an example of his success.

I went to the UNHCR office in Peshawar without the letter. I wrote a letter myself in my native language, explaining my association with David and the agency. The receptionist looked it over and asked me to wait. She said she recognized my name and thought there were already some papers here and that someone would want to speak with me. I was called inside right away for an interview.

The person who interviewed me introduced himself as Alex. Between us was an interpreter. I still had the certificate from the seminar I had attended and placed it on his desk. Alex asked me several questions and listened to me very carefully. He was a very patient person. He understood my situation. He asked me if I had any proof of my connection with the radio station starting from the year of 1994. I pulled out the small calendar with Biblical verses that was sent to me that year. It was very worn. In fact, it had been washed with my clothes, but the words were still legible. As we spoke, I think he told me, "My father is a minister. We believe in God. I listen to you from my heart, and you really need help. I can understand the situation you have." His words meant so much to me.

After a two-hour interview, he wrote "URGENT" on my application. "You must be very patient," he warned me. "There are thousands of urgent cases like yours. For now, I can provide you with a paper to show police to verify that you have a case with UNHCR. Also, I will give you some numbers in case you need help in an emergency." I felt like I could breathe for the first time in a long time.

It took all day for the paperwork to get done. Alex sent the interpreter to the cafeteria to bring me dinner. Although the food was a simple rice dish with green herbs and vegetables, it tasted so special. Was it because I was so hungry?

Alex walked through the corridor and noticed I was sitting there. He went to the cafeteria and brought back a plate for himself, sat down next to and ate with me. It was as if he understood that it was always our custom to eat with someone in order to enjoy a meal. I was eating with a spoon, and he was eating the same food with a fork. How strange!

When the paperwork was finally finished, Alex and the interpreter returned to me. Alex said, "I will be moving to a new office soon, so your case worker will be Cho." he handed me the document and explained that it was temporary. "You'll need to come back and have it renewed every two months. Best of luck to you! Be very careful!"

I didn't ask him, but I wondered why there would be another interview with another case worker. What was its purpose? I was just looking for an ID.

Chapter 22

I returned to Mirwise's home and kept busy tutoring students. Two months later, UNHCR called me for a second interview. By now it was January 2007. I went to the UNHCR again and waited for three hours before my interview with Cho. She asked me many detailed questions and sent me to a photographer in the building to get my picture taken.

I still was confused why we had so many interviews. Cho told me, "There are many, many cases. We believe your situation is dangerous because of a religious conflict. Could I ask you some questions about what you have learned about Christianity? You have a certificate, but I would like to make sure that this reflects the nature of your conflict."

"Certainly," I said.

"What did you learn that impressed you the most?"

"The first thing I learned was that Jesus said if somebody slaps you on the right side of your cheek, give him your left cheek. Also, I learned that if somebody asks you for your shirt, give them all your clothing."

"What else?"

"From the radio and my friends, I learned about the Ten Commandments."

Cho nodded her head and said that the office would

311

determine what country would accept me.

"What is this supposed to mean?" I asked. "What country?"

She smiled and said, "Your answers are acceptable."

"I still do not understand. What do you mean 'country'?"

"We are trying to send you to a different country that has freedom."

"Really?"

"Yes! We want to help you find a place where you can live freely. This is our goal. You should be safe and free."

I thought she was joking, but she was serious. I began to think about leaving for another country. I was happy to hear this news, but at that moment, I thought of my family. How could I leave them? My parents. Sima. Maryam. I knew that they were still in trouble, but I had had no contact with them for more than two years.

I was the only son my parents had, and I knew how important it was to have a son in their community. Despite the problems I had caused for my sisters, they were always happy that they had a brother. But now there would be nobody with them, and there would be nobody to support my parents. Neither of them were very healthy. Mom was sick, and dad needed help as well. What was I going to do?

I remembered what my mother and sisters said to me as I left them for the last time, "If you want us to be happy, do not come back home. Stay far away from this community. That you survive will make us happy."

In 2007, the situation in Peshawar and elsewhere got increasingly worse for the internationals. The UNHCR received a lot of threats. A bomb exploded near the UNHCR office in Peshawar. Many of the employees were told to leave the city and find refuge in the embassy.

No one from UNHCR contacted me that year. I began to think that my file might have been rejected after all. I was not able to go to the office to get my temporary document renewed, so it expired. I could not ask about my case for fear of getting arrested. After the bombing, there were always a lot of police nearby. Without that letter, I had no protection.

In 2008, there was good news. I was notified to return to the UNHCR office for another interview. The office was temporarily open again for the most urgent cases.

Cho apologized for the delay. "Your case will go very fast now," she assured me. "I encourage you to be patient. We will call you again." I waited for six more months.

During all this time, I was still living with Mirwise's family. There were frequent guests, relatives who stayed at

Mirwise's house while visiting one of the good hospitals in Peshawar. People came for one or two nights, or sometimes for a week. Sometimes, family came from far away, while other times they had guests who had come from Hangu. Word could get out back in Hangu that I was residing at the Mirwise's house. That could endanger his family.

One day I noticed that Zeba was being rather cold toward me, so I asked her what I had done.

"I am a little worried about my daughters," she explained. "People have been coming to our home to discuss engagements with our daughters, but a couple of those families have rejected the engagement, and I believe they might have made the decision because you are here. It doesn't look good. I do not want people to think that there is something wrong going on in my family, especially with my daughters' reputations at stake."

After hearing this, I felt bewildered. There was nothing I could do to solve this problem. I had no other place to live. Hotels were too expensive for me, and I didn't have the proper documents anyway.

Then Mirwise's attitude toward me changed, too. I remember that it became clear to me one night when he was sitting in a room adjacent to where his sons and I were watching a movie. It was almost midnight. I remember greeting him when he came in, but he did not respond. I was crestfallen. Was it the unacceptability of having a young man in the home with his daughters? Had I just overstayed my welcome? I tossed and turned all the night. What was I going to do? My world had become very small.

I returned to the UNHCR office. There were a lot of police and armed guards inside and outside. After the usual hassles with the guards, I got inside. Ahead of me were many other people with issues of their own. I overheard one person pleading, "We have been waiting for almost seven years, and we do not know what to do. We've lost our house."

At least three hours passed before it was my turn. I heard all the same things I had heard in the past, "You must be patient. We know your life is in danger. Please do not make any bad decisions. You must be patient for a little longer."

As I was returning home, I thought about how much my relationship with Mirwise had changed. I resolved to ask him what was going on. When I reached his street, I saw him walking home from the mosque. I ran to meet him.

"Please do not hang around here," he said. "Avoid contact with people around the area. They might ask me who you are and why you are living in my house."

"I know people are talking behind our backs," I said, "but please trust me."

"You're fine," he said. "I know you mean no harm."

"It's just that I've heard rumors lately."

"You know that I am refugee in Pakistan, and I have countless difficulties," he explained. "I am sick, and must rely on support from my in-laws in Europe. I am willing to put up with whatever for the sake of my kids so that I can keep them safe and so that they will have a decent future. I am sorry I am telling you this. You did not cause what has happened to you. Well, I don't believe you did it on purpose. God created it. But I am so worried about my family. I am wondering if I can leave the area and move to a different location. Maybe I will go back to Kabul. There is a new government over there. I am sorry. I have to ask you if you can possibly find a better place for yourself."

Now my fear was becoming a reality. I would soon have no place to live. "How would UNHCR contact me?" I wondered. They had always contacted me on Mirwise's phone. It was possible that if I were late to an interview or if I did not get a message from there that I might be stuck in this city forever. It was devastating news for me.

I recounted what I had learned at UNHCR to Mirwise. I told him that I would go there again and ask for assurance. I pleaded, "Please, allow me to stay a little longer. I will work hard tutoring. I will not spend any money for myself. I will pay rent for the room, but please do not leave yet. This is a crucial time for me."

Later, I shared my fears with Mirwise's kids. "Your dad is thinking about leaving the city soon," I said.

They said, "No. It can't be true. We will tell him not to leave yet. We will stay with you until you leave this city. You must promise to send to us some special gifts." I promised them that I would, and they ran to their parents and asked them to stay as long as necessary.

A month later, I returned to the UNHCR. The UNHCR counselor suggested, "We will call Mirwise, and let him know your case is nearly finished. Perhaps he will listen to us better than you. We promise to process your documents as soon as we can." By the time I got home, they had already called Mirwise, so I knew that the UNHCR counselors truly cared about me.

Mirwise gave me six months more to stay with him.

For the next three months there was no news. Finally, in early 2009, UNHCR called Mirwise and told him that I was accepted to go to the United States. There was a process that would begin soon and they would make contact with details. I was to attend three seminars about American culture and be interviewed at the U.S. Embassy.

Everyone began to feel more optimistic. The Mirwise's

family was looking forward to my departure, and their children were happy because I had promised them gifts. I was relieved that Mirwise would not have to put up with me for much longer. For myself, I hoped that I would finally have my own place somewhere in the world.

In March 2009, I was invited to the first U.S. culture seminar in Islamabad. The first seminar was for five days. It took place in a fancy hotel. I remember how elated I became when I was told that it was very rude in the U.S.A. to ask people about their religion. I learned that boys and girls attended school together, and men and women worked together. It was all so exciting. At the end of the seminar I was told to purchase clothing, shoes, etc., and be ready to leave.

I returned to Peshawar feeling the best I had felt in years. But I didn't tell any of the children that I'd be leaving the country. I did not want them to be sad. During this waiting period, my thoughts often turned to my family. I wanted to see them and have at least a moment with my parents and my sister to say goodbye. The thought of leaving the country without seeing them was unbearable to me, but would it be selfish to put them in danger?

Soon after I returned, officers of the ISI (Pakistan's Directorate for Inter-Services Intelligence) began to snoop around Mirwise's house. They were officially military officers, but in reality, they were no more than local rogues. They asked very personal questions about my case. I did not trust them. I did not know how they had gotten my information in the first place. Did they have connections with the U.S. Embassy? Did they talk with a guard or a police officer that had stopped me on one of my visits? To this day, I have no idea.

They demanded money. It seemed so strange to me. They said if we did not pay them, they would tell the embassy that I was associated with Taliban or that I was not really who I said I was. In short, they would prevent me from leaving. Mirwise handed over the money because he was afraid the U.S. Embassy would take back my visa.

In June, there was another seminar and an interview at the U.S Embassy. The interviewing officer's name was Marta. "I read your story," she said through a translator, "and I am so glad that you are still alive and sitting in front of me. I am also glad that you are going to the United States. Raise your right hand and state that you accept the United States law."

I raised my hand and said, "Yes."

At the end she told me, "We will be so happy if you achieve your goals there. You will have opportunities for everything. I will see you in the U.S."

I was ecstatic.

By now it was very close to 2010. I stayed in Islamabad

a while more after leaving the embassy. We had another seminar, and they booked my ticket. Then they informed me, "You have three nights before you leave the country. You must not be late to your flight. Be back here January 28th, and you will fly to Dubai, from Dubai to London, and from there to the United States."

The last instruction I remember from the embassy was, "You are not allowed to tell anyone about your visa. You should not tell anyone about when you are leaving."

I was so conflicted. How could I leave without saying goodbye to my family? I was in tears.

The only people who knew anything about my departure were Mirwise and Zeba. I had to call to tell them. I felt they had a right to know. "My visa, my ticket, everything is booked," I told them, still crying. "If I could only see my family before I go, but now it is impossible."

I returned to Peshawar by bus, crying the whole trip. When I entered the Mirwise's house for the last time, Zeba met me at the door.

"Don't look so sad," she told me. "You are about to begin a great adventure. A new chapter in your life."

"But what about my family? I feel terrible leaving them this way."

"I know that," she said as she led me to the living room.

"I know you miss your family, but don't cry." I suddenly realized the lights in the house were off.

"Is the electricity off?" I asked.

She did not look very concerned. There was a smile on her face. "I have a little going-away gift for you."

"A gift for me? Why? I can't take anything more from you. You've helped me too much already."

She turned on the lights as she said, "Here's your gift."

My mother was standing in front of me. Her beautiful face was wrapped with a white scarf on her head. I thought that I was dreaming. I ran to her and hugged her. Behind her, I saw my sister and Maryam. Tears began streaming down my face. I hugged each of them. Then I ran back to my mother to hug her again. I must have hugged each one three or four times. Then I saw my father sitting across the room. I gave him a hug and kissed his hands.

The whole family was together again after so many years. All of us were crying tears of joy, even Zeba and her family. What a grand surprise! This was the greatest gift anyone could have given me. There are no words to describe the euphoria we felt as we laughed and cried together.

Later I learned that Mirwise had found my family and invited them to his home, without telling them about me. He coaxed them there by offering a restful visit for all they had done for him and his family in the past. He even rented a car to pick them up, a big expense at such a difficult time in his family's life. On the way to his house, naturally, as they were catching up with each other's lives, I became the topic of conversation. My parents expressed to him that they felt as though they had lost their son. My mother began to cry. Father lamented, "We do not know where he is, but we are praying for him to be safe."

They were in such pain that Mirwise confessed that I'd been staying with them. "Do not worry," he consoled them. "He has been happy and productive with us. He has never forgotten you, or his sisters and cousins. He's had many bouts of homesickness. And that is why it was so important for me to bring you to him. He is leaving the country soon, and he wants to see you. I was so worried that he might take his chances to come to Hangu to see you and possibly miss his flight out of here or worse, so I brought it upon myself to bring you all together. He will be overjoyed. I am thankful I could do this small thing for you."

Unfortunately, I had such a short amount of time: I was scheduled to leave at three the next morning. Nonetheless, the whole family was together, talking, joking, and reminiscing. I managed to squeeze in some time with Maryam. She was very skinny and unhappy with her life. Sima's back had never mended, so she suffered a great deal of pain. Mother was sick.

We spent the whole night talking and did not sleep. Mirwise's family made different kinds of food. They bought sweets. The night was over, and I was sitting next to my mother. My sister was on my right side. For a moment, we were joking and laughing, and the next moment, they were crying. They made me feel very weak. Mother told me, "You have not seen any happy moments in your life. You are always in trouble." I replied, "Mom, this is good. If I were not in any trouble, where would these happy moments have come from? You see everybody is happy, and I am happy. This is a great thing. We will get together again and again."

"We are sorry that we told you not to come to our house anymore," she said. "We did this because your life is important to us."

I assured her that I had understood all along. I wanted to ask them to forgive me for all the troubles that I had caused them. I wanted to beg Sima for forgiveness; it was because of me that she had been beaten and ultimately injured. I wanted to beg my mother for forgiveness since I had not been there to help them through all their difficulties. I wanted to ask father for his forgiveness for disappointing him. He had dreamed of me becoming a doctor and a very well educated person, a brave and strong person who could make his family respected again, but I had only brought embarrassment and shame.

I knew exactly what I wanted to say, but I was unable to bring the words to my lips. I was overcome with emotion. I left the room and went outside. "Be strong," I told myself. I walked for some time and pulled myself together and returned.

I looked at my mother and my father and I knew what I needed to tell them. But I never uttered the words. And now I was leaving them and going far away. Who knew when or if I could see them again. When I approached them, tears ran down my cheeks, and I could not say anything.

I just wanted to enjoy the last day with my family. We went shopping. They bought me shoes, socks and some clothes. I knew that they did not have enough money, still, whatever they had, they put together and bought me some gifts. Maryam wanted to buy me something separately from everybody because we had been the closest of friends growing up together. Sima did the same. I told them, "I wish we were able to go together, Maryam, you, and me. We are three people that are in trouble."

Sima said, "Do not worry. If you get there, you will be able to help us. You have to leave. We are worried about you, not about ourselves. You'll never be safe here."

Mirwise's family prepared a huge dinner for us, our last

dinner together. Father was there. He looked so weak. He gave me good advice. As dinner ended, we all became aware of how little time was left before I needed to go. I realized that I had no idea when I would be able to meet my family again and suddenly the words I could not say before came easily to me. I looked first at my mom and said, "Mom, please forgive me for all the sadness that I brought to the whole family."

"We forgive you," she said. "You should not be sorry. You did what a real brother needs to do for his sisters, and what a real son has to do for his family. We are very proud of you, and our prayers will always be with you. Do not forget about us and people who helped you so much. They put their lives in danger for you. Always be thankful for the help you got from Mirwise and his family, too."

The taxi driver was at the door. Mirwise and his son took my bags out, and I said goodbye to everyone. Everyone was crying. At that moment, the strength I had gained from their love disappeared again. My tears did not stop in the taxi or at the airport. I was still not sure that I was doing the right thing. I felt again like I was dreaming.

The UNHCR representatives gave me my tickets and helped me get to the gate. They were smiling, and they told me, "Be strong. You are going to a country where you can reach your goals. You will be happy there. Good luck to you!"

I had never been on an airplane before. There were so many thoughts going through my head. As we flew I felt I was sitting on the top of a hill looking down at all the people and houses. I couldn't help thinking about the difficulties the people in those houses had. I did not want to be a selfish person worrying just about my family because, in reality, I had not spent a lot of time with them. I had left the house when I was barely seven years old. I thought of the first trip with my grandmother from Kabul to the village where there were so many sheep. And the next village and the next. And now I was on a new journey.

I had never thought that one day I would be sitting in an airplane, leaving my family and friends, going so far away. That was very difficult for me, but it was not my decision. The decision was made by the people who made the circumstances around me. I didn't want to make my family sad, but I could not regret anything I had done. At that moment, I decided to take all the happiness with me, and leave the sadness and broken parts of my life, the injuries and beatings, behind.

Then, I thought, there could be no happiness if I did not take everything with me. I was twenty-three, and a quarter of my life had been spent in that difficult situation, even though I hadn't done anything wrong. Let's keep it this way, I thought, and I will take those facts with me too.

My mind was full — overflowing — and at that point I realized that some day I would need to share my story, all of it. Maybe in that way I could help those I had left behind.

The End.

Note From The Author

I collected all the information I saw in my life and heard from my family members. I wanted to inform other parts of the world about the difficulties the women and children in Afghanistan face and how they are often forbidden to study and complete education.

Another important goal is to underscore the importance of education. From my point of view, I received injuries and rejection from my family, friends and actually from the whole area. I realized that there was no education, so they have totally wrong images in their mind about other religions. They haven't studied other religions and are in fact forbidden to study other beliefs. People don't have freedom of speech. I found out and tried to encourage people to understand each other. Most of the negative incidents and wars in the area where I came from are caused by lack of education and cultural beliefs that these clans have been kept for centuries.

The proceeds of this book will go to the children and women who still live in the shelters, so that they have an opportunity to study.

Atal RM Aryan